INTERMITTENT FASTING FOR WOMEN OVER 50

*The Complete Guide Specific for Women After 50
to Discover How to Delay Aging &
Promote Longevity, Lose Weight &
Reset Metabolism to Set a Healthy Lifestyle*

<u>WITH 150 RECIPES</u>

Amber Lane

Table of Contents

Introduction

There are so many strategies for losing weight. How do you know where to start? **Women have different needs than men** when it comes to dieting, exercise and weight loss, and it seems that many popular strategies are aimed at men who want to look like muscular bodybuilders. Many of these programs leave you hungry, unsatisfied and ultimately lead to quitting early without ever seeing results.

Intermittent Fasting (IF) is a natural way to make you feel and look better in your 50s. Your body was designed to eat in this way and has been confused by the never-ending availability of food and snacks. This form of patterned eating will restore your energy levels, retain your needed body muscle while reducing body fat and improve your overall health and wellness. The major problem with traditional diets is that they are just hard to stick to. You deny yourself your favorite food and snacks in hopes of weight loss and when you slip up, you feel ashamed and guilty, resulting in the derailment of your entire routine.

Cycling your eating pattern through periods of eating and fasting is as natural to your body as breathing. Humans have been eating this way for thousands of years, and only recently have we muddled our hunger signals so significantly that they are working against us instead of for us. Allowing yourself unrestricted access to food and snacks day in and day out alters your body's chemistry, increasing the production of hunger-signaling hormones. These hormones now tell your body constantly that you are hungry, and they are hard to ignore! Intermittent fasting will reprogram these hormones, decreasing your hunger signals and resigning them to the proper times of the day.

Changing the way you eat is also difficult. **By denying yourself your favorite meals, you are setting yourself up for failure.** Intermittent fasting allows you to enjoy your favorite foods, snacks and drinks as long as you are consuming them within your non-fasting window of time. Limiting the time you have available to consume calories will limit the total number of calories you'll ultimately consume, providing weight loss with little effort. Fasting for weight loss is different than a religious fast or fasting before a medical procedure. It does not mean you don't eat anything and wait for the pounds to fall off. You simply limit your total caloric intake during specific periods of time (hours of the day or days of the week, depending on which method of intermittent fasting you feel is most appropriate for you) while enjoying a normal diet and lifestyle the rest of the time! Reducing the amount of food you eat for short periods of time is simpler and easier to stick to for most women, resulting in success and dedication, without throwing in the towel.

The longer you practice intermittent fasting cycles, the easier you'll find them to be. Your body will adjust, you'll feel more motivation and energy and you'll wonder how you could have possibly eaten the quantity of food you used to, all day long! **This guide will explain in simple terms the science behind intermittent fasting, the benefits you can expect and how to implement the plan into your life.**

YOUR FREE GIFT

To thank you for buying this book, I would like to offer you the book **"Air Fryer Cookbook: 50 Delicious, Fast and Easy to Make Healthy Recipes"** written by a very close friend of mine, Emily Finner, who kindly allowed me to share it with you.

Air-fried foods contain up to 80% less fat in comparison to foods that are deep-fried.

With this Air Fryer Cookbook you'll discover 50 delicious easy-to-make healthy recipes using your air fryer oven. If you don't have one yet, you can look through the recipes and maybe figure out that an air fryer oven would be a nice gift for you.

FOLLOW THIS LINK

www.getYourAirFryerRecipes.com

OR SCAN THIS QR CODE WITH YOUR MOBILE

Intermittent Fasting: How It Works

Basically, fasting is defined as abstaining from eating anything. It is the deliberate action of depriving the body of any form of food for more than six hours, whereas intermittent fasting is one of its forms where the fast is carried out in a cyclic manner with the aim to reduce the overall caloric intake in a day. To most people, it may sound unhealthy and damaging for the body, but scientific research has proven that fasting can produce positive results on the human mind and body. It teaches self-discipline and fights against bad eating practices. It is basically an umbrella term that is used to define all voluntary forms of fasting. This dietary approach does not restrict the consumption of certain food items; rather, it works by reducing the overall food intake, leaving enough space to meet the essential nutrients the body needs. Therefore, it is proven to be far more effective and much easier in implementation, given that the dieter completely understands the nature and science of intermittent fasting.

Intermittent fasting is categorized into three broad methods of food abstinence, including alternate-day fasting, daily restrictions and periodic fasting. The means may vary, but the end goal of intermittent fasting remains the same, that is to achieve a better metabolism, healthy body weight and active lifestyle. The American Heart Association, AHA, has also studied intermittent fasting and its results. According to the AHA, it can help in countering insulin resistance, cardiometabolic diseases and leads to weight loss. However, a question mark remains on the sustainability of this health-effective method. The 2019 research

"Effects of intermittent fasting on health, aging and disease" has also found intermittent fasting to be effective against insulin resistance, inflammation, hypertension, obesity and dyslipidemia. However, the work on this dietary approach is still underway, and the traditional methods of fasting which existed for almost the entire human history, in every religion from Buddhism to Jainism, Orthodox Christianity, Hinduism and Islam, are studied to found relevance in today's age of science and technology.

How Does It Work

Intermittent fasting works between alternating periods of eating and fasting. It is a much more flexible approach, as there are many options to choose from according to body type, size, weight goals and nutritional needs. The human body works like a synchronized machine that requires sufficient time for self-healing and repair. When we constantly eat junk and unhealthy food without consideration of our caloric needs, it leads to obesity and toxic build-up in the body. That is why fasting comes as a natural means of detoxifying the body and providing it enough time to utilize its fat deposits.

Whatever the human body consumes is ultimately broken into glucose, which is later utilized by the cells in glycolysis to release energy. As the blood glucose level rises, insulin is produced to lower the levels and allow the liver to carry out De Novo Lipogenesis, the process in which the excess glucose is turned into glycogen and ultimately stored into fat, resulting in obesity. Intermittent fasting seems to reverse this process by deliberately creating energy deprivation, which is then fulfilled by breaking down the existing fat deposits.

Intermittent fasting works through lipolysis; though it is a natural body process, it can only be initiated when the blood glucose levels drop to a sufficiently low point. That point can be achieved through fasting and exercising. When a person cuts off the external glucose supply for several hours, the body switches to lipolysis. This process of breaking the fats also releases other by-products like ketones which are capable of reducing the oxidative stress of the body and help in its detoxification.

Mark Mattson, a neuroscientist from the Johns Hopkins Medicine University, has studied intermittent fasting for almost 25 years of his career. He laid out the workings of intermittent fasting by clarifying its clinical application and the science behind it. According to him, intermittent fasting should be chosen as a healthy lifestyle.

While discussing the application of this dietary approach, it is imperative to understand how intermittent fasting stands out from casual dieting practices. It is not mere abstinence from eating. What is eaten in this dietary lifestyle is equally important as the fasting itself. It does not result in malnutrition; rather, it promotes healthy eating along with the fast. Intermittent fasting is divided into two different states that follow one another. The cycle starts with the "Fed" state, which is followed by a "Fasting" state. The duration of the fasting state and the frequency of the fed state are established by the method of intermittent fasting. The latter is characterized by high blood glucose levels, whereas during the fasting state, the body goes through a gradual decline in glucose levels. This decline in glucose signals the pancreas and the brain to meet the body's energy needs by processing the available fat molecules. However, if the fasting state is followed by a fed state in which a person binge eats food rich in carbs and fats, it will turn out to be more hazardous for their health. Therefore, the fasting period must be accompanied by a healthy diet.

The Science Behind IF

Biologically, intermittent fasting works at many levels, from cellular levels to gene expression and body growth. In order to understand the science behind the workings of intermittent fasting, it is important to learn about the role of insulin levels, human growth hormones, cellular repair and gene expression. Intermittent fasting firstly lowers glucose levels, which in turn drops insulin levels. This lowering of insulin helps fat burning in the body, thus gradually curbing obesity and related disorders. Controlled levels of insulin are also responsible for preventing diabetes and insulin resistance. On the other hand, intermittent fasting boosts the production of human growth hormones up to five times. The increased production of HGH aids quick fat burning and muscle formation.

During the fasting state, the body goes into the process of self-healing at cellular levels, thus removing the unwanted, non-functional cells and debris. This creates a cleansing effect that directly or indirectly nourishes the body and allows it to grow under reduced oxidative stress. Likewise, fasting even affects the gene expression within the human body. The cell functions according to the coding and decoding of the gene's expression; when this transcription occurs at a normal pace in a healthy environment, it automatically translates into the longevity of the cells, and fasting ensures unhindered transcription. Thus, intermittent fasting fights aging, cancer and boosts the immune system by strengthening the body cells.

Pros and Cons

The different dietary examples have gotten consideration as an approach to reach and keep up a solid weight and to pick up wellbeing benefits even in effectively sound people.

Research is progressing to completely comprehend the upsides and downsides of intermittent fasting. Long-term studies are missing to know without a doubt if this eating style gives enduring advantages.

Pros

Simple to Follow

Numerous dietary examples center on eating specific foods and restricting or keeping away from different food sources. Learning the particular standards of an eating style can require a significant time duty. For instance, there are whole books committed to understanding the fasting diet or figuring out how to follow a Mediterranean-style feast plan. On an eating plan that joins Intermittent fasting, you just eat as indicated by the hour of day or day of the week. When you've figured out which intermittent fasting convention is best for you, all you need is a watch or a schedule to realize when to eat.

No Calorie Counting

As anyone might expect, individuals who are attempting to reach or keep up a sound weight for the most part like to maintain a strategic distance from calorie tallying. While nutrition names are effectively found on numerous foods, the way toward estimating segment measures and organizing day-by-day tallies either physically or on a cell phone application can be dull.

An investigation carried out in 2011 found that individuals are bound to follow plans when all pre-estimated calorie-controlled foods are provided. Commercial eating diets, for example, WW, Jenny Craig and others offer these types of assistance for a charge. Nonetheless, numerous individuals don't have the resources to pay for these kinds of projects, particularly in the long haul. Intermittent fasting gives a basic elective where practically no calorie-checking is required. Much of the time, calorie limitation (and along these lines, weight loss) happens in light of the fact that food is either eliminated or essentially limited on specific days or during specific hours of the day.

No Macronutrient Limitations

There are well-known eating plans that essentially confine explicit macronutrients. For instance, numerous individuals who follow low-carb eating tend to support wellbeing or get in shape. Others follow a low-fat eating diet for restorative or weight loss purposes. Every one of these projects requires the shopper to embrace another method for eating, regularly supplanting most loved foods with new and perhaps different food sources. This may require new cooking abilities and figuring out how to shop and stock the kitchen in an unexpected way.

None of these abilities are required when intermittent fasting basically because there is no objective macronutrient extend and no macronutrient is limited or taboo.

Unrestricted Eating

Any individual who has ever changed their eating routine to accomplish a health advantage or arrive at a solid weight realizes that you begin to desire foods that you are advised not to eat. Indeed, an investigation distributed in 2017 affirmed that an expanded drive to eat is a key factor during a weight loss plan.

In any case, this test is explicitly constrained on an Intermittent Fasting plan. Nourishment limitation just happens during certain restricted hours and on the non-fasting hours or days of the plan, you can, by and large, eat anything you desire. Truth be told, specialists here and there call these days "consuming" days.

Obviously, proceeding to eat undesirable foods may not be the most advantageous approach to pick up profits by Intermittent fasting, however, removing them during specific days constrains your general intake and may at last give benefits.

Might Boost Longevity

One of the most broadly referred advantages of intermittent fasting includes life span. As indicated by the National Institute on Aging, studies in rats have demonstrated that when mice are put on plans that seriously confine calories (regularly during fasting periods) many demonstrated an augmentation of life expectancy and diminished paces of a few ailments, particularly malignant growths.

So, does this advantage reach out to people? As per the individuals who advance the eating diets, it does. Nonetheless, long-term studies are expected to affirm the advantage. As indicated by a survey distributed in 2010, there has been observational research connecting strict fasting to long-haul life span benefits, yet it was difficult to decide whether fasting gave the advantage or whenever related variables had an impact.

Advance Weight Loss

In a survey of intermittent fasting research distributed in 2018, creators report that the examinations they inspected indicated a huge diminishing in fat mass among subjects who took an interest in clinical preliminaries. They additionally saw that intermittent fasting was found as productive in decreasing weight, regardless of the weight list. It is conceivable, in any case, that IF is not any more powerful than conventional calorie limitation. Intermittent fasting might not be any more compelling than different weight control plans that confine calories all the time. A recent report contrasted intermittent fasting and customary eating diets (characterized as constant energy limitation) and found that weight loss benefits are comparable. It is likewise conceivable that weight loss results may rely upon age. An examination distributed in the diary Nutrition in 2018 inspected the impacts of intermittent fasting (time-limited benefiting from) youthful (20-year-old) versus more established (50-

year-elderly people) men. Intermittent fasting somewhat diminished weight in the youthful, however not in the more established men. Nonetheless, muscle power remained the equivalent in the two groups.

Glucose Control

In 2018, some intermittent fasting specialists recommended that this eating style may help those with type 2 diabetes oversee glucose. In any case, the discoveries have been conflicting.

Nonetheless, another investigation distributed in 2019 indicated a less amazing effect on blood glucose control. Scientists led a two-year follow-up of a year mediation contrasting intermittent fasting and persistent calorie limitation in individuals with type 2 diabetes. They found that HbA1c levels expanded in both the constant calorie limitation and intermittent fasting at two years. These discoveries were reliable with results from different investigations demonstrating that, notwithstanding the scope of dietary mediations, it isn't unprecedented for blood glucose levels to increment after some time in those with type 2 diabetes. The examination creators do note, notwithstanding, that Intermittent energy limitation might be better than ceaseless energy limitation for keeping up lower HbA1c levels, yet noticed that more investigations are expected to affirm the advantage.

Cons

Side Effects

Studies exploring the advantages of Intermittent fasting additionally point to certain symptoms that may happen during the fasting phase of the eating program.

For instance, it isn't remarkable to feel grouchy, tired and experience cerebral pains when your calories are seriously limited. Almost certainly, these reactions will happen when food is altogether dispensed with (for instance, during programs like substitute day fasting) and more averse to happen when nourishment intake is diminished, (for example, on the 5:2 eating diet when 500–600 calories are devoured during fasting days).

Decreased Physical Activity

One eminent reaction of intermittent fasting might be the decrease in physical activity. Most Intermittent fasting programs do exclude a suggestion for physical movement. Of course, the individuals who follow the projects may encounter enough exhaustion that they neglect to meet everyday step objectives and may even change their ordinary exercise schedules.

Proceeding with investigations has been proposed to perceive how intermittent fasting may influence physical action plans.

Extreme Hunger

As anyone might expect, it is regular for those in the fasting phase of an IF diet intends to encounter serious appetite. This craving may turn out to be increasingly outrageous when they are around other people who are consuming common dinners and bites.

Medications

Numerous individuals who take meds locate that taking their solution with food assists with soothing certain symptoms. Truth be told, a few meds explicitly convey the proposal that they ought to be taken with food. Hence, taking meds during fasting might be a test.

Any individual who takes drugs ought to address their medicinal services supplier before beginning an IF plan to be certain that the fasting stage won't meddle with the prescription's viability or symptoms.

No Focus on Nutritious Eating

The foundation of most intermittent fasting programs is timing, instead of food decision. Along these lines, no foods (counting those that need great nutrition) are completely eliminated and foods that give great nutrition are not promoted. Hence, those following the eating diet don't really figure out how to eat a solid eating diet.

May Promote Overeating

During the "devouring" phase of numerous intermittent fasting plans, feast size and supper recurrence are not limited. Rather, users appreciate a not indispensable eating diet. Sadly, this may promote indulging in certain individuals. For instance, if you feel denied following a day of complete fasting, you may feel slanted to indulge (or eat inappropriate foods) on days when "devouring" is permitted

Long-Term Limitations

While the act of intermittent fasting isn't new, a great part of the investigation exploring the advantages of this eating style is moderately later. Consequently, it is difficult to discern whether the advantages are durable. Furthermore, specialists regularly remark that long-term studies are expected to decide whether the eating plan is even safe for over a while.

Until further notice, the most secure strategy is to work with your human services supplier when picking and beginning an IF program. Your social insurance group can screen your advancement, including medical advantages and worries to ensure that the eating style is solid for you.

Possible Negative Effects of IF

Even though we can't overlook the way that irregular fasting has a lot of medical advantages. There are significantly more favorable circumstances that are extraordinary for the human body and increment the life expectancy of people, too. There are likewise some negative effects of intermittent fasting. Any individual who is going to begin irregular fasting at any point shortly has to know both the positive and negative effects of fasting and afterward choose whether it's advantageous for your body or not.

Anxiety Attacks

Another potential side effect of detoxing through intermittent fasting is the potential for an anxiety attack. This can happen when you are withholding food for an extended period of time, especially if you are new to intermittent fasting.

An anxiety attack may come upon you because you feel that you are not getting enough nutrition, or you are missing your usual feeding times.

Digestive Distress

Since intermittent fasting has a detoxing component to it, you may experience digestive distress during your first few experiences. This is due to your body flushing out much of the residual matter in your body in addition to simply excreting whatever is still left over in the digestive tract.

While this is normal to a certain extent, care should be taken if you happen to experience severe diarrhea. This may be especially true if you jump into a fasting period after overeating the previous day. As long as it isn't anything that you feel to be abnormal, then you can attribute it to the detoxing process. However, if symptoms do not subside, then you may need to seek medical attention at once.

You Might Struggle to Maintain Blood Sugar Levels

Although the intermittent fasting diet tends to improve blood sugar levels in most people, this is not always true for everyone. Some people who are eating following the intermittent fasting diet may find that their ability to maintain a healthy blood sugar level is compromised.

The reason why this happens varies. For some people, not eating frequently enough may encourage this to happen. For others, transitioning too quickly or taking on too intense of a fasting cycle too soon can result in a shock to the body that causes a strange fluctuation in blood sugar levels.

You Might Experience Hormonal Imbalances
A certain degree of fasting, especially when you build up to it, can support you in having healthier hormone levels. However, for some people, intermittent fasting may lead to an unhealthy imbalance of hormones. This can result in a whole slew of different hormone-based symptoms, such as headaches, fatigue and even menstrual problems in women.

Again, the reason for the hormonal imbalance varies. For some people, particularly those who are already at risk of experiencing hormonal imbalances, intermittent fasting can trigger these imbalances to take place. For others, it could go back to what they are consuming during the eating windows. Eating meals that are not rich in nutrients and vitamins can result in you not having enough nutrition to support your hormonal levels.

If you begin experiencing hormonal imbalances when you eat the intermittent fasting diet, it is essential that you stop and consult your doctor right away. Discovering where the shortcomings are and how you can correct them is vital. Having imbalanced hormones for too long can lead to diseases and illnesses that require constant life-long attention.

Headaches
A decrease in your blood sugar level and the release of stress hormones by your brain as a result of going without food are possible causes of headaches during the fasting window. Problems may also be a clear message from your body telling you that you are very low on water and getting dehydrated. This may happen if you are completely engrossed in your daily activities and you forget to drink the required amount of water your body needs during fasting.

To handle headaches, ensure you stay well hydrated throughout your fasting window. Keep in mind that exceeding the required amount of water per day may also result in adverse effects. Reducing your stress level can also keep headaches away.

Cravings

During your fasting periods, you might find that you have higher levels of desire than usual. This often happens because you are telling yourself that you cannot have any food, so suddenly you start craving many different foods. This is because all you are thinking about is food. As you think about food, you will begin to think about the different types of food that you like and that you want. Then, the cravings start.

Early on, you may also find yourself craving more sweets or carbs because your body is searching for an energy hit through glucose. While you do not want to have excessive levels of sugar during your eating window, as this is bad for blood sugar, you can always have some. The ability to satisfy your cravings is one of the benefits of eating a diet that is not as restrictive as some other foods are.

Low Energy

A feeling of lethargy is not uncommon during fasting, especially at the start. This is your body's natural reaction to switching its source of energy from glucose in your meals to fat stored in your body. So, expect to feel a little less energized in your first few weeks of starting with intermittent fasting. To troubleshoot the feeling of lethargy, try as much as possible to stay away from overly strenuous activities. Keep things low-key. Spending more time sleeping or just relaxing is another right way to ensure that your energy reserves are not depleted too quickly. The first few weeks are not the time to test your limits or push yourself.

Foul Mood

You may find yourself being on edge during fasting, even if you are someone who is naturally predisposed to being good-natured. The reason for the feeling of edginess is straightforward. You are hungry, yet you won't eat, and you are struggling to keep your cravings in check, plus, you may already be feeling tired and sluggish. Add all of these to the internal hormone changes due to the sharp decline in your blood sugar levels, and it's no wonder why you may be in such a foul mood. Tempers can easily flare up and you may be quick to become irritated. This is normal when beginning a fasting lifestyle.

Excess Urination

Fasting tends to make you visit the bathroom more frequently than usual. This is an expected side effect since you are drinking more water and other liquids than before. Avoiding water to reduce the number of times you use the bathroom is not a good idea at all, no matter how you look at it. Cutting down water intake while you are fasting will make your body become dehydrated very quickly. If that happens, losing weight will be the least of your problems. Whatever you do, do not avoid drinking water when you are fasting. Doing that is paving the way for a humongous health disaster waiting to happen. You don't want to do that.

Heartburn, Bloating and Constipation

Your stomach is responsible for producing stomach acid, which is used to break down food and trigger the digestion process. When you eat frequent meals, unusually large meals, regularly, your body is used to producing high amounts of stomach acid to break down your food. As you transition to a fasting diet, your stomach has to get used to not producing as much stomach acid.

You might also notice an increase in constipation and bloating. People who eat regularly consume high amounts of fiber and proteins that support a healthy digestion process. When you switch to the intermittent fasting cycle, you can still eat a high volume of fiber and protein. However, early on, you might find that you forget to. As you discover the right eating habits that work for you, it may take some time for you to get used to finding ways to work in enough fiber and protein to keep your digestion flowing.

Heartburn may not be a widespread adverse effect, but it does sometimes occur in some people. Your stomach produces highly-concentrated acids to help break down the foods you consume. But when you are fasting, there is no food in your stomach to be broken down, even though acids have already been produced for that purpose. This may lead to heartburn.

Bloating and constipation usually go hand in hand and can be very discomforting to individuals who suffer from it due to fasting.

Heeding the advice to drink adequate amounts of water usually keeps bloating and constipation in check. Heartburn typically resolves itself quickly, but you can take an antacid tablet or two if it persists. You may also consider eating fewer spicy foods when you break your fast.

You Might Start Feeling Cold

As you begin to adjust to your intermittent fasting diet, you might find that your fingers and toes get quite cold. This happens because blood flow towards your fat stores is increasing, so blood flow to your extremities reduces slightly. This supports your body in moving fat to your muscles so that it can be burned as fuel to keep your energy levels up.

You Might Find Yourself Overeating

The chances for overeating during the break of the fast are high, especially for beginners. Understandably, you will feel starving after going without food for longer than you are used to. It is this hunger that causes some people to eat hurriedly and surpass their standard meal size and average caloric intake. For others, overeating may be a result of an uncontrollable appetite. Hunger may push some people to prepare too much food for breaking their fast, and if they don't have a grip on their desire, they will continue to eat even when they are satiated. Overeating or binging when you break your fast will make it difficult to reach your goal of optimal health and fitness.

Hunger Pangs

People who start intermittent fasting may initially feel quite hungry. This is especially common if you are the type of person who tends to eat regular meals daily.

If you start feeling hungry, you can choose to wait it out if you have an eating window right around the corner. However, if there is a more extended waiting period or you are feeling excessively hungry, you should eat. Feeling hungry to the point that it becomes uncomfortable or distracting is not helpful and will not support you in successfully taking on the intermittent fasting diet. This is a pronounced side effect of going without food for longer than you are accustomed to.

The Body Changes in Women Over 50

Menopause is one of the most complicated phases in a woman's life. The time when our bodies begin to change and important natural transitions occur that are too often negatively affected, while it is important to learn how to change our eating habits and eating patterns appropriately. In fact, it often happens that a woman is not ready for this new condition and experiences it with a feeling of defeat as an inevitable sign of time passing, and this feeling of prostration turns out to be too invasive and involves many aspects of one's stomach.

It is therefore important to remain calm as soon as there are messages about the first signs of change in our human body, to ward off the beginning of menopause for the right purpose and to minimize the negative effects of suffering, especially in the early days. Even during this difficult transition, targeted nutrition can be very beneficial.

What Happens to the Body of a Menopausal Woman?

It must be said that a balanced diet has been carried out in life and there are no major weight fluctuations, this will no doubt be a factor that supports women who are going through menopause, but that it is not a sufficient condition to present with classic symptoms that are felt, which can be classified according to the period experienced. In fact, we can distinguish between the pre-menopausal phase, which lasts around 45 to 50 years, and is physiologically compatible with a drastic reduction in the production of the hormone estrogen (responsible for the menstrual cycle, which actually starts irregularly). This period is accompanied by a series of complex and highly subjective endocrine changes. Compare effectively: headache, depression, anxiety and sleep disorders.

When someone enters actual menopause, estrogen hormone production decreases even more dramatically, the range of the symptoms widens, leading to large amounts of the hormone, for example, to a certain class called catecholamine adrenaline. The result of these changes is a dangerous heat wave, increased sweating and the presence of tachycardia, which can be more or less severe.

However, the changes also affect the female genital organs, with the volume of the breasts, uterus and ovaries decreasing. The mucous membranes become less active and vaginal dryness increases. There may also be changes in bone balance, with decreased calcium intake and increased mobilization at the expense of the skeletal system. Because of this, there is a lack of continuous bone formation, and conversely, erosion begins, which is a predisposition for osteoporosis.

Although menopause causes major changes that greatly change a woman's body and soul, metabolism is one of the worst. In fact, during menopause, the absorption and accumulation of sugars and triglycerides changes and it is easy to increase some clinical values such as cholesterol and triglycerides, which lead to high blood pressure or arteriosclerosis. In addition, many women often complain of disturbing circulatory disorders and local edema, especially in the stomach. It also makes weight gain easier, even though you haven't changed your eating habits.

The Ideal Diet for Menopause

In cases where disorders related to the arrival of menopause become difficult to manage, drug or natural therapy under medical supervision may be necessary. The contribution given by a correct diet at this time can be considerable, in fact, given the profound variables that come into play, it is necessary to modify our food routine, both in order not to be surprised by all these changes, and to adapt in the most natural way possible.

The problem of fat accumulation in the abdominal area is always caused by the drop in estrogen. In fact, they are also responsible for the classic hourglass shape of most women, which consists of depositing fat mainly on the hips, which begins to fail with menopause. As a result, we go from a gynoid condition to an android one, with an adipose increase localized on the belly. In addition, the metabolic rate of disposal is reduced, this means that even if you do not change your diet and eat the same quantities of food as you always have, you could experience weight gain, which will be more marked in the presence of bad habits or irregular diet.

The digestion is also slower and intestinal function becomes more complicated. This further contributes to swelling as well as the occurrence of intolerance and digestive disorders which have never been disturbed before. Therefore, the beginning will be more problematic and difficult to manage during this period. The distribution of nutrients must be different: reducing the amount of low carbohydrate, which is always preferred not to be purified, helps avoid the peak of insulin and at the same time, maintains stable blood sugar.

Furthermore, it will be necessary to slightly increase the quantity of both animal and vegetable proteins; choose good fats, preferring seeds and extra virgin olive oil and severely limit saturated fatty acids (those of animal origin such as grease, fat, etc.). All this to try to increase the proportion of antioxidants taken, which will help to counteract the effect of free radicals, whose concentration begins to increase during this period. It will be necessary to prefer foods rich in phytoestrogens, which will help to control the states of stress to which the body is subjected and which will favor, at least in part, the overall estrogenic balance.

These molecules are divided into three main groups and the foods that contain them should never be missing on our tables: isoflavones, present mainly in legumes such as soy and red clover; lignans, of which flax seeds and oily seeds, in general, are particularly rich; coumestan, found in sunflower seeds, beans and sprouts. A calcium supplementation will be necessary through cheeses such as parmesan; dairy products such as yogurt, egg yolk, some vegetables such as rocket, Brussels sprouts, broccoli, spinach, asparagus; legumes; dried fruit such as nuts, almonds, or dried grapes.

Excellent additional habits that will help to regain well-being may be: limiting sweets to sporadic occasions, thus drastically reducing sugars (for example, by giving up sugar in coffee and getting used to drinking it bitterly); learn how to dose alcohol a lot (avoiding spirits, liqueurs and aperitif drinks) and choose only one glass of good wine when you are in company, this because it tends to increase visceral fat which is precisely what is going to settle at the abdominal level. Clearly, even by eating lots of fruit, it is difficult to reach a high carbohydrate quota as in a traditional diet. However, a dietary plan to follow can be useful to have a more precise indication on how to distribute the foods. Obviously, one's diet must be structured in a personal way, based on specific metabolic needs and one's lifestyle.

Perimenopause

There are many ways to lose weight during perimenopause, such as intuitive eating, a low-carb diet, a ketogenic diet and more. If you are experiencing menopausal symptoms along with an unhealthy lifestyle (i.e., high intake of carbs, sugar, or processed foods), then you may need help in other areas as well (exercising regularly) before choosing an approach. Trying several different approaches may lead you to the ideal approach for your body and life stage.

Understanding your perimenopausal symptoms will help you determine which dietary approach and exercise regimen is best for you. If you find any of the following signs, then these should be your first concern:

- Aging or weight gain
- Significant mood swings or depression
- Low libido, hot flashes, night sweats, or difficulty sleeping
- Difficulty concentrating, memory loss, impatience and irritability
- Constantly tired or needing caffeine after lunch to wake up in the afternoon

These are not all of the signs associated with perimenopause, there are many others.

Why Intermittent Fasting Over 50?

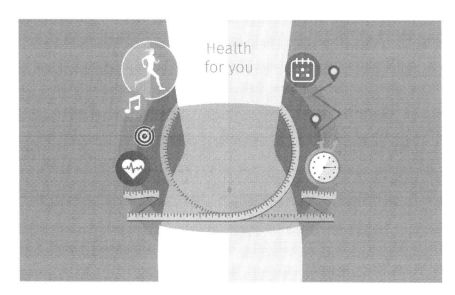

Women's obesity can trigger several diseases and intermittent fasting can help prevent them. Additionally, if you are over 50, intermittent fasting will help you balance these aspects of your life.

Hypertension

Hypertension is a condition when blood pressure is elevated. When a woman becomes aged, her blood vessels become less elastic. The system that keeps the body's blood in place is stressed as a result of this. That could explain why almost two-thirds of women over 50 have high blood pressure. Weight loss through intermittent fasting is the most effective way to treat hypertension.

Diabetes

Diabetes is a medical condition that affects at least one in every ten women. The likelihood of developing the disease rises as you get older. Excess weight can cause diabetic disorders such as heart failure, blindness, kidney dysfunction and other health problems.

Condition of the Heart

Plaque forming in the arteries as a result of excessive eating is a major cause of heart disease. It starts in childhood and gets worse as one grows older. Heart disease affects many men and 5.6 % of women in the United States between 40 and 58. Fasting or eating a balanced diet are safe ways to control cardiovascular problems.

Obesity

Obesity is a problem that affects many people. It is not about gaining a few extra pounds if one weighs too much for one height; it is about one's health. Stroke, asthma, cancer, arthritis, coronary disease and elevated blood pressure are among the more than 20 chronic diseases attributed to obesity. Obesity affects at least 30% of the elderly population.

Arthritis

The extreme wear and tear of time were once specifically traced by doctors to this disease of the joints, and it certainly is a factor. However, genetics and lifestyle are expected to play a significant role. Past joint injuries may have been caused by a lack of physical activity, dementia, or being overweight.

Osteoporosis

Bones weaken with age, particularly in women, which can lead to fractures. It impacts 53.9 million Americans over the age of 50. A healthy diet rich in calcium and vitamin D, weight loss by fasting, or daily weight-bearing exercises such as jogging, cycling and climbing stairs are all helpful.

Cancers and Tumor

Cancer is the primary cause of death in old age. Young people are also affected by the condition, but your chances of having it more than double between 46 and 54. You have little control of a person's age or chromosomes, but you do have control over alcohol and lead an unhealthy lifestyle. Fasting over different amounts of time has also helped older adults minimize their risk of serious diseases, with much of the literature focused on cancer's positive effect. Fasting tends to suppress certain cancer-causing mechanisms and can also slow tumor growth, according to the report.

Menopause

Hot flashes, vaginal dryness, night sweats, mood swings, insomnia, burning and itching are all classic symptoms of menopause. Heart disease and osteoporosis tend to intensify as women reach menopause. People also begin fasting for extended periods to treat both the long and short effects of menopause. Belly fat is a big problem for many postmenopausal women, not just for beauty but also for fitness. The reduction of belly fat caused by intermittent fasting helped women reduce their risk of metabolic syndrome, a category of health issues that increase the risk of heart disease and diabetes in postmenopausal women.

Types of Intermittent Fasting

In order to harness and manipulate autophagy to benefit your body, you need to be able to upregulate its functioning within your cells. There are various ways to do this, and we will look at these ways, as well as how they work so that you can better understand how they work to affect your body. By upregulating autophagy, you are able to make your body resistant to many diseases.

Water Fasting

The first type of fasting we will look at is water fasting. Water fasting is a method of fasting in which a person does not ingest anything except water for a period of time. Many people practice water fasting for periods up to 72 hours, but this is a decision that should be made with the help of a doctor.

If you have ever gone into the hospital for a medical procedure, they likely told you that you could not eat food and could only drink water for a certain amount of time before the procedure. This practice would have been a form of water fasting. Some people also try water fasting as a method of "detoxing" their bodies. Another use for it though is to manually induce autophagy. Many people practice periods of water fasting to induce autophagy in order to rid their bodies of potentially harmful viruses or bacteria in an effort to reduce their risk of diseases such as cancer and Alzheimer's and even increase their lifespan. This is because of the cleansing properties of autophagy, as it breaks down infected cells and uses their salvageable parts for new and healthy cells to be generated. Autophagy can reduce the risk of cancers because of the way that it clears the body of damaged cells, which could otherwise accumulate and develop into cancer.

There are added benefits of water fasting that do not directly involve autophagy but are worth noting anyway. Water fasting has been shown to reduce blood pressure, cholesterol and even improve the functioning of insulin in the body, therefore improving blood sugar.

The problem with water fasting is that it can be quite dangerous if not practiced in a safe and monitored way. Consult a doctor before attempting water fast so that you can ensure you are doing so in a safe way. There are some groups of people who should not practice water fasting. These groups include pregnant women, children, the elderly and people with eating disorders.

Another thing to keep in mind when attempting water fast in an effort to lose weight is that the weight lost during a water fast may not be the exact type of weight that you are trying to lose. During a water fast, there is a severe restriction in calories, which leads to the breakdown of fat stores, but some of the weight loss could also include water weight, stored carbohydrates and sometimes muscle (in longer fasts). What this means is that after a water fast, the weight loss may come back quite quickly if the majority were water or carbohydrate stores, as these are replenished very quickly once a person begins eating again. If this is the case, do not be concerned, this is a very normal reaction for your body to have as it is built to anticipate unexpected fasts and therefore has ways to protect you from these, such as storing carbohydrates.

When approaching a water fast, it is beneficial to prepare your body for a few days leading up to it by tapering off your eating portions in order to gradually remove food from your day. This will better prepare your body to go without food for a day or two. Another way to get your body prepared to water fast is to fast for part of the day so that it can get accustomed to spending some time without food. You may also be wondering how a water fast could make you lose water weight, but it is entirely possible and even likely. This is because much of the water we bring into our bodies throughout the day is enclosed in the foods we eat. If your water intake remains the same, but your food ingestion dramatically decreases, you could end up becoming dehydrated and thus losing water weight.

You will also need to adjust your activities to accommodate this water fast, especially if it is your first time trying it. If you are not used to fasting, you may feel dizzy or light-headed, and this may make some of your daily tasks more difficult. This could be due to lower blood sugar or lower blood pressure if you are dehydrated. Be sure to keep this in mind as you attempt a water fast and be sure to increase your water intake to avoid a drop in blood pressure.

There is still much more research that needs to be done surrounding water fasting in humans in particular. Water fasting as a method of weight loss is a relatively new approach and one that is just beginning to be explored with human test subjects.

16 And 8

This is the method where you would eat for 8 hours of the day and fast for 16 hours. When doing this method of IF, you would usually skip breakfast and eat between the hours of 1 pm and 9 pm, or 12 noon and 8 pm. The hours you choose can vary depending on your work schedule and your lifestyle, but the key is that you eat for 8 hours of the day and have a longer portion of the day in which you are fasting. This is the most popular method of IF and is the easiest if you are new to following specific diets. Many people will naturally eat during an 8-hour window of the day if they do not tend to eat breakfast, which is why this method is the easiest to transition to. Some people prefer to use different ranges of hours, but in terms of research, 16 and 8 have been shown to be the most effective. If you are looking for something a little different, we will look at the two next most common methods below.

5:2

This method is different from the other two in that it involves a number of calories instead of hours. However, similar to the previous method, you are breaking up your week into different days instead of breaking up your day into hours.

In this method, you will restrict your caloric intake to between 500 and 600 calories on two days of the week. This is similar to the Eat-Stop-Eat method, except that instead of fully fasting on Monday and Thursday (for example), you will greatly restrict your caloric intake. For the other five days of the week, you will eat as you normally would. This is a method of intermittent eating, though it does not involve complete fasting. This method would be good for those who are unable to completely fast for two days of the week but who want to try a form of intermittent eating still. For example, this would be a good option for someone who works a physically laborious job and who cannot be feeling light-headed during the workday.

Eat-Stop-Eat

This method is a little different than the 16 and 8 methods, as instead of breaking the day up into hours, you would be breaking your week up into days. You would fast for either one or two days of the week, not on back-to-back days. For example, you would fast from after lunch on Monday until after lunch on Tuesday and then again beginning after lunch on Thursday. For all the other days of the week, you could normally eat as you wish. This type is similar to water fasting in that it is a period of time where you are fasting, which is 24 hours in length. However, it is intermittent in that it only lasts 24 hours and repeats itself twice every week consistently. Water fast could be a one-off for 72 hours.

With this method, you will have to keep in mind that what you choose to eat and in what quantities on the days that you are not fasting will have effects on the results you see. You want to ensure you are not bingeing on the days that you are not fasting. This method is a good choice for those who prefer more flexibility during their eating times and do not want to restrict their eating to a small 8-hour window of the day, namely those who want to eat breakfast. This could be good for those who have longer working days and who prefer to have a longer time to eat during the day.

Alternate Day Fasting

This method of fasting involves fasting every other day and eating normally on the non-fasting days. Similar to other forms of IF, you are able to drink as much as you want calorie-free drinks such as black coffee, tea and water. You would fast for 24 hours on your fasting days, for example, from before dinner on one day until before dinner the next day. This method can be very successful or very unsuccessful depending on the person. The problem with this method is that it can lead to bingeing on the non-fasting days. If, however, you are a person that does not tend to binge, you may enjoy the flexibility that this diet offers by allowing you to eat whatever you want on alternating days.

There is a modification that some people choose to apply to this form of IF, where they allow themselves to eat 500 calories on their fasting days. This works out to about 20-25% of an adult person's daily energy needs, which will still put you in an extreme calorie deficit for those days, leading to the induction of autophagy. This method allows a person to continue with this diet consistently for a longer period of time than they may be able to with full fasts. It has the same effectiveness and works better with our modern lifestyles.

This type of IF has been shown to be very beneficial for weight loss and is a good choice for those who have weight loss as their main priority. Because of the calorie deficit that it put a person into, they are using more energy than they are putting into their body, which leads to a breakdown of fat stores and weight loss.

Women-Specific Methods of Intermittent Fasting

There is some evidence that suggests that Intermittent Fasting affects the bodies of men and women differently. The bodies of women are much more sensitive to small-calorie changes, especially small negative changes in the intake of calories. Since the bodies of women are made for conceiving and growing babies, women's bodies must be sensitive to any sort of changes that may occur in the internal environment of the body to a larger degree than the bodies of men, in order to ensure that it will produce healthy and strong progeny. For this reason, however, some women may have trouble practicing intermittent fasting according to the above methods.

These methods may involve too much restriction for the body of a woman, and she may feel some negative effects such as light-headedness or fatigue. In order to prevent this, there are some adjusted methods of intermittent fasting that will work better for women's bodies. This is not to say that women cannot practice IF or fasting of any sort, but that they must keep this in mind when deciding to try a fasting diet. Women can take a modified approach to fasting so that the internal environment of their bodies remains healthy. There are some slightly different patterns of IF that may be safer and more beneficial for women. We will look at these below.

Crescendo

This method is quite similar to the Eat-Stop-Eat method, except that in this one, the hours have been changed slightly. This fasting regimen involves breaking up the week into days as well as breaking up the days into hours. In this case, the woman should fast for 14 to 16 hours of the day twice a week and eat normally every other day. These fasting days would not be back to back and would not be more than twice per week.

Alternate Day 5:2

Alternatively, she could fast every other day but only for 12-14 hours, eating normally on the days in between. On the fasting days, she would eat 25% of her normal calorie intake, making it a reduction in calories and not a full-blown fast.

14 And 10

In this method, the day would be broken up into segments of hours. The woman would fast for 14 hours of the day and eat for 10 hours. Beginning with this modified version will allow her body to become used to fasting. Eventually, when she is comfortable with it, she can change the hours by one hour per day in order to reach 16 and 8.

By reducing the hours of the fast to 14 hours or less, women can still experience the benefits that IF can have for weight loss and autophagy induction without putting themselves in any danger. This is not to say that women cannot fast in the same way that men can, but that they must start off slowly and gradually increase their hours of fasting so that they do not shock their bodies. When it comes to health, we must acknowledge the fact that the bodies of men and women are built differently and thus will respond differently to changes.

12 And 12

Women can also benefit from reducing their fasting window even further to 12 hours. This method can be beneficial in the beginning while your body gets used to the fasting and you can gradually work your way up from here. In this method, you would normally only eat until three hours before you go to sleep and then you could begin eating again early enough in the morning to have your first meal be breakfast. For example, if you go to bed at 10 pm, you would only eat until 7 pm. Then you could eat breakfast after 7 am. This is beneficial for people who like to eat breakfast and who do not like to begin their day fasted.

For any person, regardless of their sex, the best approach to fasting may vary. When it comes to choosing an approach, being flexible is important. With dieting, the most important factor is consistency and so the best diet that you can choose for yourself will be the one that you can consistently maintain for a long enough period of time so your body can adjust and changes can begin to occur.

Find Out Your Intermittent Fasting Plan

With this section, we are going to help you understand exactly how to identify the best plan for intermittent fasting protocol. Something to realize would be that intimate fasting can be customized based on your needs. In case you're trying to have eating schedules based on your lifestyle, then chances are intermittent fasting is the solution for you. As you realize by now, there are a lot of ways for you to follow intermittent fasting. We talked about the different intermittent fasting protocols and which one will benefit you in what way. One thing to remember is that you will still see many of the benefits we discussed in the previous chapters, regardless of the plan you follow. This means that following intermittent fasting or certain protocol should not demotivate you when it comes to following a certain plan.

Now that you are aware of the different methods of intermittent fasting that are available to you, it is time to choose one. When choosing a method for yourself, there are a few things to keep in mind. You will need to ask yourself several questions when choosing an intermittent fasting schedule for yourself. Below, I will show you the questions that you need to ask yourself in order to determine which method of intermittent fasting will fit best with your life.

1. **What Does My Current Daily Schedule Look Like?**

Take a look at your daily and weekly schedules. This will give you insight into what your busiest times of the day are and when you will need energy the most.

2. **When Am I Currently Fasting?**

Everyone is fasting while they are sleeping. Do you normally wake up and wait to eat until lunch? Do you eat early in the morning, but have a very small dinner? Any extended period of time without eating is considered a fast or even a mini fast. Pinpoint these times so that you can incorporate a fasting schedule that will not disrupt your current lifestyle too much. For example, if you usually skip breakfast and eat lunch around noon, then you would have been fasting from the time you last ate the night before until noon the next day (as long as you had nothing but water, black coffee, or black tea during that time). For this person, I would recommend a 16/8 or some variation of this as they are already following something quite similar.

3. When Can I Not Afford to Fast?

If you have specific commitments that require your energy, such as an after-dinner sports club or early morning meetings, keep these in mind when choosing your method. You likely wouldn't want to skip dinner if you have evening commitments that require physical exertion, or if you have morning meetings, then eating breakfast first may be what you need in order to hit the ground running in the morning. If you are a person that has both of these, then maybe you will need to fast for 24 hours on the weekend when you have a less demanding schedule, as you need all the energy that food gives you throughout the week.

4. Can I Fast for a 24-Hour Period?

Not everyone can fast for 24 hours without some experience or an entire day put aside where they can relax while fasting. Are you able to put in the time and effort that a 24-hour fast requires, and are you able to deal with the side effects that could come with it, such as lethargy, irritability, headaches and so on? If so, this method could work for you. If not, it is best to choose another.

5. What Are the Demands in My Life That May Cause Challenges?

Having children that you have to care for and cook for may pose a challenge when it comes to intermittent fasting. So can an exercise or sports regimen, a plethora of social events, or a lack of time to adequately prepare a meal plan. Take all of these challenges into account so that you are ready to handle them all. Plan ahead so that nothing comes as a surprise, and you will be able to stay on track even when these challenges inevitably present themselves.

After you have answered all of the questions above, you will have a better idea of what intermittent fasting plan will fit best into your life. The one that fits the best with the lifestyle you already lead will be the least likely to stick and lead to successful results.

Remember, the first one you choose does not have to be the one you stick to forever. If it doesn't work for you for any reason, you can always tweak the hours, the days, or even try a different one completely. As long as it is an intermittent fasting schedule, it will lead to autophagy (which we will look at soon) and thus the positive results that you are looking for.

Now, you have to remember that we can only go through certain lifestyles and scenarios. Don't expect us to have a perfect scenario for you. You will have to decide that for yourself once you're done reading this chapter. However, all the scenarios should be close to the scenario you are living in. If we suggest a certain intermittent fasting protocol based on the scenarios, make sure that you still try on all the intermittent fasting protocols and realize which one works for you. The truth is, the best personal trainer is the best nutritionist you're going to have. Once you start understanding your body, you will be in a better position to utilize intermittent fasting at its full potential, but you also have a great idea of went to stop and when you should begin.

If that makes sense, then you should be steps ahead of your trainers and nutritionists, which you might hire. We are not saying that you should not have a personal trainer or nutritionist, what we are saying is that you will be in a much better position if you can understand how your body functions to create a customized plan for you. Now, the first scenario we are going to be using would be very similar to someone who works in a 9-to-5 job. If you're someone who works from 9 to 5 and only gets one lunch break during the day and chances are 16/8 intermittent fasting would be ideal. To clarify, you can always start with a 12/12 intermittent fasting protocol, in the beginning, to get ready. However, once you get your feet wet with intermittent fasting, you should go with the 16/8 method.

The 16/8 method works well for people who work a 9-to-5 job because it is straightforward to manage. The beauty of the 16/8 method when it comes to intermittent fasting is that you can set the hours to whatever time you want to eat and you don't want to eat. For example, many people notice better brain functioning when they are not eating any food. This means you can skip breakfast and not eat throughout the whole workday allowing you to focus on the task. Then once you're done working, you can have yourself a nice big breakfast. We know numerous amounts of people doing this, and not only did they notice they lost a lot of weight, but they also got a lot better at the work which they are performing. The beauty of intermittent fasting is that it allows you to lose body fat and give you the mental clarity you're looking for.

The reason why you get mental Clarity is that you will not be spiking up your insulin throughout the day. When you spike up your insulin, you will notice things such as lethargy and overall laziness. This's why the 16/8 method works great when it comes to recovering some issues you could be facing when it comes to brain fatigue or brain fog. That being said, start with the 12/12 method and slowly build up to the 16/8 method to see better results. In this scenario, your work performance will not only go up, but you also lose a lot of weight and get the overall health benefits you're looking for when it comes to intermittent fasting. This will work especially well for people who are above the age of 50.

The reason why it will work a lot better for people who are above this age is simply that they will go through a phase known as autophagy. Autophagy has been shown to reduce many health complications, including the slowing down of aging. This makes it ideal for people looking to slow down aging. So, if you work a 9-to-5 job and are looking to lose body fat while slowing down aging, then we recommend that you follow the 16/8 method throughout the workday, meaning the fastest route to the workday, and have yourself a nice breakfast after you're done working. I want you to perform a lot better at your workplace and see better results overall when it comes to intermittent fasting and losing body fat. Keep in mind that the scenario we talked about is the first scenario that most people will be going through.

However, we have a ton of scenarios to talk about. Now, chances are there will be a lot of people who work in labor, looking to reap the benefits of intermittent fasting. If you are working labor, chances are it will be a little bit more difficult for you to continue with intermittent passing. However, with the right scheduling in the right planning, you should have no problem concerning intermittent fasting. Now let's say you work the labor 8 hours a day. What we would recommend is trying to have most of your calories throughout the 8-hour window. Once you are done with your work, make sure that you start your fast right away.

Now, there are a lot of ways for you to get your calories throughout your eating window while you are working. You can have things such as protein shake, and you are quickly going to have a pre-prepared meal, which will help you to consume all the calories you need throughout the whole day. We recommend that you eat throughout the day while you're working because a labor job could be tedious. We want to make sure that you don't paint or affect your work in any way possible. This is why we recommend you follow the 16/8 method and include your eating window while working. Many people who work in labor tend to follow this protocol because it works so well. That's because they won't get all the calories they need when they need it. You need to have a good steady flow of food intake while you are physically working.

Your body can only break down fat quickly, which is why a good amount of carbohydrates and nutrients is important when you're performing anything physical. That being said, you can always resort to the 5/2 method when you are intermittent fasting. If you don't like the 16/8 method, then you can always follow the 5/2 method. This method works great as you only have to "fast" for two days out of the week, meaning you can normally eat when you are working. As you get older, especially in the labor workforce, you will be required to be well-fed when working. The last thing we want is for you to have injuries at your workplace. That being said, you can either follow the 16/8 method or go right ahead and follow the 5/2 method fasting on your non-working days.

This will allow you to see the results that you're looking for when it comes to anti-aging, regardless of the fasting protocol you follow. However, if we're honest, the 16/8 method works a lot better when it comes to seeing results regarding intermittent fasting and anti-aging. Now, let's pick out another scenario, let's talk about someone who works the night shift. If you're someone who works the night shift, the chances are that you will be in a much better scenario than a lot of people. You will be in a much better position than a lot of people because nightshift tends to be slow for most cases. If you're a nurse, then chances are you will have no time to eat any food.

So, the best thing for you to do would be not to have any food during your shift, and once you're done your shift, you can have more food allowing you to be a lot better at fasting. The great thing about being a nurse or working a night shift is that you will have a much better position of not only continued with intermittent fasting but also the desire to not eat. Numerous times we have heard nurses talk about not having the time to eat, or simply not in the mood for eating anything.

Having this mentality will help you tremendously to continue with intermittent fasting, which is why it is so important to understand which intermittent fasting protocol works for your needs. Fasting said if you're a nurse who is working night shifts, the best-case scenario for you would be to fast through your whole shift and have your eating window once you've done your work. For instance, let's say you work 10 hours a day, then fast for 10 hours a day and eat the rest of the time. This gets a little bit tricky for a nurse, as the hours can sometimes be scattered or sometimes not an ideal case scenario for you to fast.

However, the best way to go about fasting is, if you're a nurse who works a shift at a very demanding job, we recommend you fast during the time you are working. This will allow you to be in a perfect position when it comes to fasting and to see the best results overall with intermittent fasting. In essence, you will be trying out all the types of intermittent fasting when you are working the night shift or working as a nurse, for example. Depending on your shift, you will be fasting either 10 hours or even up to 24 hours, depending on how you feel. That being said, this will give you the best possible scenario for you to continue with intermittent fasting and make it a habit. Many people don't realize it, but making intermittent fasting a part of your life is much more important than looking to follow a specific plan.

We have given you enough scenarios to figure out which plan would work best for you based on your lifestyle. Now we will move on and talk about all the methods and which deliver the specific goal that you're looking for. Keep in mind that all these plans will work tremendously well if you're looking to slow down aging and to lose body fat overall feeling better about yourself. However, we will break down all the plans so that you can better decide which one to pick and finalize.

• **16/8**: As you know, the 16/8 method is one of the most popular ways when it comes to intermittent fasting. The 16/8 method will help you lose body fat, but it will also help you with the anti-aging process and improve your overall function. Many people follow this method as it is the most convenient method to follow and comfortably flexible.

Depending on your lifestyle, this method could work very well when it comes to giving you the results that you're looking for.

This method's beauty is that you can build muscle, lose fat and do anything you want while making this a life choice. When I say a life choice, you can follow this plan for the rest of your life and not feel taxed out. If it is feasible for you, we recommend that you follow the 16/8 method, one of the most studied ways of intermittent fasting.

- **12/12**: Now, this method is for someone looking to set up intermittent fasting without going too hard. If you don't know how intermittent fasting works or you don't know if it is going to be the right path for you, then you should start with the 12/12 method. This method will allow you to get your feet wet when it comes to intermittent fasting so that you can continue with intermittent fasting if you enjoy it or make it a bit more challenging by upping the fasting times.

That being said, the 12/12 method is merely something to get your feet wet with and not something you should do for the rest of your life. The secure troll's method is a great plan to start. However, you will not see the anti-aging effects or the weight loss effects that you're looking for following this method. In the beginning, you will, however, as you go along, you will not see the results that you are looking for when it comes to losing body fat are slowing down the aging process. This is where the 16/8 method will shine, as it will give you enough time to fast while seeing the benefits that you are hoping to get out of intermittent fasting.

- **The water fast**: Now, water fast is for someone looking to detoxify their body, but they're changing the way their body functions. This plan is only to be followed a handful of times to detoxify their gut, so they digest a lot better. As you might know, the stomach is known as the second brain. It is known as a second brain because your body heavily depends on your gut and how it digests, as you know, eating food is necessary for living, which is why we must take care of the organs, especially our gut. Make sure you use this method to clean out your organs and to see better results from it. This will allow you to be in a better position when it comes to digesting food and keeping your organs beautiful and safe.

- **5:2 Diet**: This fasting protocol is ideal for people who are looking to lose weight quickly. Now, if you're someone who wants to lose weight rapidly and has the motivation and willpower to get it done, then the 5/2 works the best. A disciple makes you lose a lot of body fat and a short period, allowing you to live a lot better overall.

Now, keep in mind that following the 5/2 diet will not help you with any anti-aging process long-term. But I will help you detoxify your body and make you lose a ton of weight, especially in the beginning. Don't follow this protocol for the rest of your life as it is not sustainable. However, once you get the hang of this plan, you will be in a much better position to lose fat and get your goal weight quicker than you would. Once you've lost a way to find the 5/2 diet, we recommend following the 16/8 diet quickly. The 16/8 diet is where you want to be when it comes to see long-lasting results. Nonetheless, a 5/2 diet will work for you if you do a labor job, because of the structure.

Keep in mind that we want you to use your brain when it comes to picking out the right plan. As always, make sure that you know your body before you start following any of these plans. We recommend a start off with a 12/12 method as you will see significant benefits from it initially. However, once you get your feet wet with intermittent fasting, then we recommend that you start following other plans that will help you achieve that goal as well.

12 Myths About IF to Dispel

Issues that are not popular can be misunderstood with a lot of misconceptions and myths surrounding them. Intermittent fasting is one such issue. Many people with half-baked information suddenly become experts on the topic and are always willing to give advice to anyone willing to listen. It doesn't matter how long a false premise is considered correct, once the evidence is present, the error is exposed and wise people will know to stick with the facts.

Myth #1: Intermittent Fasting Is Unsafe for Older Adults

Anyone can engage in intermittent fasting as long as they do not have any medical conditions and are not pregnant or lactating. Of course, our bodies do not all have the same tolerance levels even in people that look exactly alike. If one or more persons respond negatively to intermittent fasting because they are advanced in age and are women, it does not mean that another will react the same way.

There is no doubt that intermittent fasting is not meant for everyone. Fasting is not safe for children because they need all the food they can get for continual development. Fasting in itself is not an issue for older people, any adult can fast.

Myth #2: You Gain Weight as You Age

A myth is a combination of facts and falsehood. This is a typical example of that. It is saying that growing older means your metabolism will slow down and your body will not burn or use up calories as fast as when you were younger. However, weight gain in older adults is not a given. The key to keeping your body performing optimally is to develop and maintain healthy habits such as fasting intermittently, drinking enough water, reducing stress levels and getting adequate exercise.

Myth #3: Your Metabolism Slows Down During Fasting

This myth represents one of those big misunderstandings I mentioned earlier. The difference between calorie restriction and deliberately choosing when to take in calories is huge. Intermittent fasting does not necessarily limit calorie intake neither does it make you starve. It is when a person starves or undereats that changes occur in their metabolic rate. But there is no change whatsoever in your metabolism when you delay eating for a few hours by fasting intermittently.

Myth #4: You Will Get Fat if You Skip Breakfast

"Breakfast is the most important meal of the day!" This is one of the most popular urban myths about intermittent fasting. It is in the same category with the myths, "Santa doesn't give you presents if your naughty" and "carrots give you night vision." Some people will readily point to a relative or friend who is fat because they don't eat breakfast. But the question is: are they fat because they don't eat breakfast? Or do they skip breakfast because they are fat and want to reduce their calorie intake?

The best way to collect unbiased data when conducting scientific studies is through randomized controlled trials (RTC). After a careful study of 13 different RTCs on the relationship between weight gain and eating or skipping breakfast, researchers from Melbourne, Australia found that both overweight and normal-weight participants who ate breakfast gained more weight than participants who skipped breakfast. The researchers also found that there's a higher rate of calorie consumption later in the day in participants who ate breakfast. This puts a hole in the popular notion that skipping breakfast will make people overeat later in the day (Harvard Medical School, 2019).

The truth is, there is nothing spectacular about eating breakfast as far as weight management is concerned. There is limited scientific evidence disproving or supporting the idea that breakfast influences weight. Instead, studies only show that there is no difference in weight loss or gain when one eats or skips breakfast.

Myth #5: Exercise Is Harmful to Older Adults Especially While Fasting

No. It is not harmful to exercise while fasting. And no, exercise is not harmful to older adults, whether they are fasting or not. On the contrary, exercising during your fasting window helps to burn stored fats in the body. When you perform physical activities after eating, your body tries to burn off new calories that are ingested from your meal. But when you exercise on an empty or nearly empty stomach, your body burns fats that are stored already and keeps you fit.

What is harmful to older adults is not engaging in exercises at all. A lack of exercise or adequate physical activity in older adults is linked to diabetes, heart disease and obesity among other health conditions.

Researchers from Harvard Medical School demonstrated in a landmark study that frail and old women could regain functional loss through resistance exercise (Harvard Medical School, 2007). For ten weeks, participants from a nursing home (100 women aged between 72 and 98) performed resistance exercises three times a week. At the end of 10 weeks, the participants could walk faster, further, climb more stairs and lift a great deal of weight than their inactive counterparts. Also, a 10-year study of healthy aging by researchers with the MacArthur Study of Aging in America found that older adults (people between 70 and 80 years) can get physically fit whether or not they have been exercising at their younger age. The bottom line is, as long as you can move the muscles in your body, do it because it is safe and will only help you live a better and longer life.

Myth #6: Eating Frequently Reduces Hunger

There is mixed scientific evidence in this regard. Some studies show that eating frequently reduces hunger in some people. On the other hand, other studies show the exact opposite. Interestingly, at least one study shows no difference in the frequency of eating and how it influences hunger (US National Library of Medicine, 2013). Eating can help some people get over cravings and excessive hunger, but there is no shred of evidence to prove that it applies to everyone.

Myth #7: You Can't Teach an Old Dog New Tricks

The brain never stops learning neither does it stop developing at any age. New neural pathways are created when a person learns something new at any age. And with continued repetition, the neural pathways become stronger until the behavior is habitual. Older people are often more persistent and have a higher motivation than younger people when it comes to learning new things. Learning should be a lifelong pursuit and not an activity reserved for young people.

Don't allow anyone to convince you into believing that it is too late to learn new eating habits because you are in your golden years or are approaching it. It doesn't matter if you've never tried fasting, you can still train your brain to make fasting a habit even in old age. Start small, make it a natural occurrence in everyday life, repeating until you get used to it, and your positive results aka glowing skin, improved energy will motivate you to make it into a lifestyle.

Myth #8: You Must Lose Weight During Intermittent Fasting

This myth is rooted in the hype that intermittent fasting has received in recent years. Unless done correctly, intermittent fasting may not yield weight loss benefits. For you to experience any significant loss in weight, you must ensure that you eat healthily during your eating window. Equally, it is important to stick to the fasting schedule. If you keep cheating and adjusting your fasting window to favor more eating time or you overeat during the eating window to compensate for lost meals, your chances of losing weight will be greatly diminished.

Myth #9: Your Body Will Go into "Starvation Mode" If You Practice Intermittent Fasting

This myth is based on the misconception of what starvation mode is and what triggers it. First of all, starvation is when your body senses that there is a significant drop in energy supply and reduces your metabolic rate. In simple terms, it is a reduction in the rate at which your body burns fat as a lack of food. This is an automatic response to conserve energy. It makes sense to reduce energy consumption if there is little to no supply of further energy coming from meals. In other words, if you stay away from food for too long, your body activates the starvation mode and significantly stops any further loss of body fat.

Having said that, intermittent fasting does not trigger starvation mode. Instead, intermittent fasting helps to increase your metabolic activities. Meaning, your body can burn more fat when you fast for short periods. Starvation mode is only triggered when you engage in prolonged fasting over 48 hours, a practice I do not recommend for older adults.

Myth #10: An Aging Skin is Better Taken Care of with Anti-Aging Cream

This is not necessarily true. Brown spots, sagging skin and wrinkles can indeed be reversed using expensive creams and topical treatments especially if a dermatologist prescribes them. These topical products exfoliate the top layer of your skin and make them appear smoother. However, that result (clear, smooth skin) is only a temporary effect.

A better way to look younger without any side effects is by activating autophagy. Engaging in mild stress-inducing activities, such as intermittent fasting and exercising, is the way. One key element to maintaining healthy skin is quenching your skin's thirst. Not drinking enough water can damage the skin causing it to become dry, blemished and lead to wrinkles. Drinking adequate amounts of water every day is the best approach to successfully "take the years off."

Myth #11: Fasting Deprives Your Brain of Adequate Dietary Glucose

Some people believe that your brain will underperform if you don't eat foods rich in carbohydrates. This myth is rooted in the notion that your brain uses only glucose as its fuel. But your brain doesn't use only dietary glucose for fuel. Some very low-carb diets can cause your body to produce ketone bodies from high-fat foods. Your brain can function well on ketone bodies. Continuous, intermittent fasting coupled with exercise can trigger the production of ketone bodies. Additionally, your body can also use a process known as gluconeogenesis to produce the sugar needed by your brain. This means that your body can effectively produce it on its own without you feeding it with just carbs.

Intermittent fasting does not interfere with brain function or its fuel or energy needs. However, because intermittent fasting is not suitable for everyone, if you feel shaky, dizzy, or extremely fatigued during fasting, consider talking with your doctor or reducing your fasting window.

Myth #12: Intermittent Fasting Will Make Older Adults Lose Their Muscle

First of all, it is stereotypical and largely incorrect to think of older people as frail. Frailty is not limited to just older adults and is a generalization of old age. Younger people can become frail if they suffer from a disabling chronic disease or have a poor diet. Scientists studied data from almost half a million people and found that middle-aged adults as young as 37 show signs of frailty (Mail Online, 2018).

Food to Eat and to Avoid During IF

What to Eat

Berries
Berries are very healthy, incredibly flavorful and much lower in calories and sugar than you might think! Their tart sweetness can really bring a smoothie to life and they make an absolutely delicious snack on their own without any help from things like cream or sugar.

Cruciferous Vegetables
These are the vegetables like cabbage, Brussels sprouts, broccoli and cauliflower. These are wonderful additions to your diet because they're packed with vital nutrients and with fiber that your body will love and use with quickness!

Eggs
Eggs are such a great addition to your diet because they're packed to the gills with protein, you can do just about anything with them, they're easy to prepare, they travel well if you hard boil them and they can pair with just about anything. They're a great protein source for salads and they're good on their own as well.

Fish
Fish is a wonderful source of protein and healthy fats. Whitefish, in particular, is typically very lean, but fish like salmon that have a little bit of color in them are packed with protein, fats and oils that are great for you. They're good for brain and heart health, and there's a huge array of delicious things you can do with them.

Healthy Starches Like Certain Potatoes (with Skins!)
Red potatoes, in particular, are perfectly fine to eat, even if you're trying to lose weight because your body can use those carbs for fuel and the skins are packed with minerals that your body will enjoy. A little bit of potato here and there can do good things for your nutrition, but they are also a great way to feel like you're getting a little more of those fun foods that you should cut back on.

Legumes

Beans, beans, the magical fruit. They're packed with protein and the starch in them just makes them stick to your ribs without making you pay for it later. They're wonderful in soups, salads and just about any other meal of the day that you're looking to fill out. By adding beans to your regimen, you might find that your meals stick with you a little bit longer and leave you feeling more satisfied than you thought possible.

Nuts

I know you've heard people talking about how a handful of almonds makes a great snack and if you're anything like me, you've always had kind of a hard time believing it. Nuts, as it turns out, have a good deal of their own healthy fats in them that your body can use to get through those rough patches and, while they are not the most satisfying snack on their own, you might consider topping your salad with them for a little bit of crunch, or pairing them with some berries to make them a little more satisfying.

Probiotics to Help Boost Your Gut Health

Probiotics can be found in a number of different ways in health food stores, but they can make digestion and gut health much more optimum. Having a happy gut often means that your dietary success and overall health will improve!

Vegetables That Are Rich in Healthy Fats

Not to sound topical or trendy, but avocados are a great example of a vegetable that is packed with healthy fats. Look for vegetables with fatty acids and a higher fat content and you will find that if you add more of those into your regimen, you will get hungry less often.

Water, Water, Water and More Water

No matter what you decide to add to or subtract from your regimen, stay hydrated. This will aid in digestive health and ease, it will keep you from feeling slumpy or tired, and it will keep you from getting too hungry. Add electrolytes where you need to and don't be shy about bringing a bottle with you when you go from place to place. Stay hydrated!

What to Avoid

Grains

While grains may have their health benefits and be full of fiber, you can also get these nutrients elsewhere. The human diet does not require grain consumption. The truth is while grains may have some benefits, they are ridiculously high in both total and net carbohydrates, making them incompatible with the ketogenic diet. A single serving of brown rice contains a shocking 42 net carbs, which is almost double your net carb intake for an entire day.

Although some people do try what is known as the targeted ketogenic diet, which is a version of the diet specifically designed for those who complete extended and strenuous workouts. With the targeted ketogenic diet, a person will consume a small serving of a carb-heavy food, such as grains, 30 to 40 minutes before working out.

Starchy Vegetables and Legumes

Some vegetables are high in carbohydrates. This includes potatoes, beans, beets, corn and more. Yes, these vegetables may have nutritional benefits, but you can get these same nutrients in low-carb vegetable alternatives. To put into perspective how high in carbs these options can be, a medium-sized white potato contains 43 net carbs (more than a serving of brown rice!), a standard sweet potato contains 23 net carbs, and a serving of black beans contains 25 net carbs.

Sugary Fruits

Most fruits have high sugar content, meaning that they are also high in carbohydrates, which will spike your blood sugar and cause an insulin reaction. To avoid this, it is important to avoid most fruits. The exception is that you can enjoy berries, lemons and limes in moderation. Some people will also enjoy a small serving of melon as a treat from time to time, but watch your portion size as it can add up quickly!

Milk and Low-Fat Dairy Products

As you can enjoy dairy products such as cheese on the ketogenic diet, you may consider trying milk. Sadly, milk is much higher in carbohydrates than cheese, with a glass of two-percent milk containing 12 carbs, half of your daily total. Instead, choose low-carb and dairy-free milk alternatives such as almond, coconut and soy milk.

You may consider using low-fat cheeses instead of full fat to reduce the saturated fats you are consuming. But, if you are looking to reduce your saturated fat intake, choose lighter cuts of meat rather than low-fat dairy products. The reason for this is because when the cheese is made with low-fat dairy, it naturally has a higher carbohydrate content, which will cut into your daily net carb total.

Cashews, Pistachios and Chestnuts

While you can enjoy nuts and seeds in moderation, keep in mind that nuts contain a moderate level of carbohydrates, and therefore should be eaten in moderation. However, some nuts are high in carbs and thus are not fed on the ketogenic diet, including cashews, pistachios and chestnuts.

If you want to enjoy nuts, instead of these options, you can fully enjoy almonds, pecans, walnuts, macadamia nuts and other options.

Most Natural Sweeteners

While you can certainly enjoy sugar-free natural sweeteners such as stevia, monk fruit and sugar alcohols, you should avoid natural sweeteners that contain sugar. Suffice to say the sugar content makes these sweeteners naturally high in carbs. Not only that but, they will also spike your blood sugar and insulin. This means you should avoid things such as honey, agave, maple, coconut palm sugar and dates.

Alcohol

Alcohol is not generally enjoyed on the ketogenic diet, as your body will be unable to burn off calories while your liver attempts to process alcohol. Many people also find that when they are in a state of ketosis, they get drunk more quickly and experience more severe hangovers. Not only that, but alcohol adds unnecessary calories and carbohydrates to your diet.

The worst offenders to choose would be margaritas, piña coladas, sangrias, Bloody Mary, whiskey sours, cosmopolitans and regular beers.

But, if you do choose to drink alcohol regardless, drink in moderation and choose low-carb versions, such as rum, vodka, tequila, whiskey, and gin. The next best options would be dry wines and light beers.

Proven Tips for Managing Your Fast

Intermittent fasting doesn't have to be a struggle. In fact, if done right, it can be quite enjoyable, even life-changing. It's all just a matter of how you approach your fast. You've just got to do what you can to make the best of it. Having said that, here in this chapter, we will go over some tips and tricks to get you on the right path and ensure that you have a successful fast.

Don't Get Bored

One of the biggest pitfalls of intermittent fasting is boredom. Mindless eating, after all, often strikes simply because we don't have anything else to do. The more packed your itinerary is, the less likely you will succumb to eating out of sheer boredom. If you have a hobby, make full use of it. Blow off some steam with a pastime rather than mindlessly grazing through an afternoon. Just make sure that you don't get bored and you will be more likely to stay on track.

Satisfy Your Appetite with Zero-Calorie Beverages

Simply drinking water or some other zero-calorie beverage can help temporarily fill you up and satisfy your appetite while you fast. Water, of course, is a good and filling zero-calorie beverage. It's nature's replenisher. But it's not the only one. Some good zero-calorie beverages include:

- Coffee (without cream or sugar)

- Springwater

- Tea (again, without cream or sugar)

Don't Get Overwhelmed

Many who start a regimen of intermittent fasting - especially if they have no previous experience with fasting - find themselves becoming a bit overwhelmed. Going into a fasting routine stressed out will only make things worse, however, whatever you do, make sure you don't stress out over your efforts. In order to avoid this, go into your intermittent fasting routine with the attitude that it's okay to make mistakes. If you slip up the first couple of times you fast, don't worry about it, just correct yourself and try again. Intermittent fasting after all - in many ways - is a trial and error process. You need to experiment and figure out exactly what works best for you, so be sure to give yourself enough breathing room to do so.

Have a Good Attitude

In many ways, this might seem like common sense, but it's worth saying regardless (attitude is everything). If you go into intermittent fasting with the attitude that you are going to fail, then it probably won't be long before you conclude a self-fulfilled prophecy. On the other hand, if you take on a good attitude of trying to be positive and make the best of things, you will be that much closer to success. It's really just as simple as that. And if you aren't in a good mood. Just fake it until you make it and your spirits will begin to rise regardless.

Make Use of BCAAs

Just what are BCAAs you might ask? That fancy little acronym stands for "Branch Chain Amino Acids," and they are highly useful when it comes to girding your system for an intermittent fast. Among other things, BCAAs make sure that you do not lose too much muscle while your body is burning up all of that fat during a fast. And studies have shown that taking 10 g of a BCAA supplement before a fast can indeed really do some wonders.

Fast While You Sleep

Unless you are engaged in an intermittent fast that takes up a whole 24-hour period, it's always advisable to situate most of your fast time during your sleeping hours. This means you could usually simply skip dinner or breakfast, and then sleep off the rest of your fast. If for example, you want to fast for 16 hours, you could have an early evening meal at 5 pm and then not eat again until 9 am the next morning. This would thereby complete a 16-hour fasting cycle without much feeling of deprivation involved. Just fast while you sleep and your body will do the rest.

Use Proper Portion Control

When it comes to successful intermittent fasting, being able to use proper portion control is crucial. If your fast-day routine allows you to eat under 500 calories, portion control is of course necessary in order to keep yourself within your allotted limits. But perhaps even more importantly, should be the portion control you exercise when it comes to your non-fast days. For it is the non-fast day that will have you tempted to go overboard and eat too much if you are not careful.

Intermittent fasting, after all, recommends someone to fast, then normally eat, not fast and then binge! Because believe me, if someone starves themselves for 24 hours and then eats until they are absolutely stuffed the next day—they're not helping anyone! But there is a simple physiological reason that folks tend to get messed up when it comes to their portion control after a fast. You may notice that after the first few hours of a fast, you cease to feel hungry.

Hunger pains are the body's built-in cue to eat. You may notice, however, that after the first few hours of a fast, your hunger subsides. This is because, by then, our body realizes that food is not forthcoming. For the rest of your fast, you may very well not feel all that hungry at all. But this is what happens folks. After you end your fast and get out a bowl of pasta, the second you take that first bite, your body screams, "Oh wow, we have food now!"

And almost immediately the hunger pains hit you with abandon, and your body is now working you overtime to consume as much as you possibly can. It's just the way we are hardwired to be. Everything about the human condition is geared toward survival and our ancestors in the past went through periods of feast and famine, often not knowing when the next meal was going to be. So it is that our body will turn off the hunger signal when we do without for a while, and yet will then poke, prod and goad us into eating as much as possible when food is suddenly available.

That's great for someone who might not know when their next meal might be, but it's horrible for someone trying to plan a strategic intermittent fast under strict guidelines and protocol. That's why sometimes you might find yourself having to exercise a bit of mind over matter in order to keep yourself from overdoing it on your non-fast day and proper portion control can be a real lifesaver when it comes to intermittent fasting.

Closely Monitor Your Results

For most of us, nothing serves to encourage us more than seeing good, positive results. And as you fast, being able to monitor your progress will not only help you to improve problem areas, it will also give you a boost of self-confidence to show you how far you have come along in the process. Also, as intermittent fasting is in many ways a trial and error process, being able to track your journey in real-time enables you to tweak and finesse your experience until your methodology is at its most optimal. Everyone is different after all, and intermittent fasting isn't a one-size-fits-all program. Having said that, monitoring your results will give you the feedback you need to make improvements when necessary, as well as provide you with solid encouragement as you go.

Mistakes to Avoid

When you are looking to make any significant adjustments in your life, it can take time to discover exactly how to do it in the best ways possible. Many people will make mistakes and have some setbacks as they seek to improve their health through intermittent fasting. Some of these mistakes are minor and can easily be overcome, whereas others may be dangerous and could cause serious repercussions if they are not caught in time.

In this chapter, we are going to explore common mistakes that people tend to make when they are on the intermittent fasting diet. We will also explore why these mistakes are made and how they can be avoided. It is important that you read through this chapter before you actually commit to the diet itself. That way, you can ensure that you are avoiding any potential mistakes beforehand. This will help you in avoiding unwanted problems and achieving your results with greater success and fewer setbacks.

You should also keep this chapter handy as you embark on your intermittent fasting diet. That way, if you do begin to notice that things are not going as you had hoped, you can easily reflect back on this chapter and get the information that you need to adjust your diet and improve your results.

Switching Too Fast

A significant number of people fail to comply with their new diets because they attempt to go too hard too fast. Trying to jump too quickly can result in you feeling too extreme of a departure from your normal. As a result, both psychologically and physically, you are put under a significant amount of stress from your new diet. This can lead to you feeling like the diet is not actually effective and like you are suffering more than you are actually benefitting from it.

If you are someone who eats regularly and who frequently snacks, switching to the intermittent fasting diet will take time and patience. I cannot stress the importance of your transition period enough.

It is not uncommon to want to jump off the deep end when you are making a lifestyle change. Often, we want to experience great results right away and we are excited about the switch. However, after a few days, it can feel stressful. Because you didn't give your mind and body enough time to adapt to the changes, you ditch your new diet in favor of things that are more comfortable.

Fasting is something that should always be acclimated to over a period of time. There is no set period, it needs to be done based on what feels right for you and your body. If you are not properly listening to your body and its needs, you are going to end up suffering in major ways. Especially with diets like intermittent fasting, letting yourself adapt to the changes and listening to your body's needs can ensure that you are not neglecting your body in favor of strictly following someone else's guide on what to do.

Choosing the Wrong Plan for Your Lifestyle

It is not uncommon to forget the importance of picking a fasting cycle that actually fits with your lifestyle and then fitting it in. Trying to fast to a cycle that does not fit with your lifestyle will ultimately result in you feeling inconvenienced by your diet and struggling to maintain it.

Often, the way we naturally eat is in accordance with what we feel fits into our lifestyle in the best way possible. So, if you look at your present diet and notice that there are a lot of convenience meals and they happen all throughout the day, you can conclude two things: you are busy, and you eat when you can. Picking a diet that allows you to eat when you can is important in helping you stick to it. It is also important that you begin searching for healthier convenience options so that you can get the most out of your diet.

Anytime you make a lifestyle change, such as with your diet, you need to consider what your lifestyle actually is. In an ideal world, you may be able to completely adapt everything to suit your dreamy needs. However, in the real world, there are likely many aspects of your lifestyle that are simply not practical to adjust. Picking a diet that suits your lifestyle rather than picking a lifestyle that suits your diet makes far more sense.

Taking the time to actually document what your present eating habits are like before you embark on your intermittent fasting diet is a great way to begin. Focus on what you are already eating and how often and consider diets that will serve your lifestyle. You should also consider your activity levels and how much food you truly need at certain times of the day. For example, if you have a spin class every morning, fasting until noon might not be a good idea as you could end up hungry and exhausted after your class. Choosing the dieting pattern that fits your lifestyle will help you actually maintain your diet so you can continue receiving great results from it.

Eating Too Much or Not Enough

Focusing on what you are eating and how much you are eating is important. This is one of the biggest reasons why a gradual and intentional transition can be helpful. If you are used to eating throughout the entire day, attempting to eat the same amount in a shorter window can be challenging. You may find yourself feeling stuffed and far too full to actually sustain that amount of eating on a day-to-day basis. As a result, you may find yourself not eating enough.

If you are new to intermittent fasting and you take the leap too quickly, it is not unusual to find yourself scarfing down as much food as you possibly can the moment your eating window opens back up. As a result, you find yourself feeling sick, too full and uncomfortable. Your body also struggles to process and digest that much food after having been fasting for any given period of time. This can be even harder on your body if you have been using a more intense fast and then you stuff yourself. If you find yourself doing this, it may be a sign that you have transitioned too quickly and that you need to slow down and back off.

You might also find yourself not eating enough. Attempting to eat the same amount that you typically eat in 12-16 hours in just 8-12 hours can be challenging. It may not sound so drastic on paper, but if you are not hungry, you may simply not feel like eating. As a result, you may feel compelled to skip meals. This can lead to you not getting enough calories and nutrition on a daily basis. In the end, you find yourself not eating enough and feeling unsatisfied during your fasting windows.

The best way to combat this is to begin practicing making calorie-dense foods before you actually start intermittent fasting. Learning what recipes you can make and how much each meal needs to have in order to help you reach your goals is a great way to get yourself ready and show yourself what it truly takes to succeed. Then, begin gradually shortening your eating window and giving yourself the time to work up to eating enough during those eating windows without overeating. In the end, you will find yourself feeling amazing and not feeling unsatisfied or overeating as you maintain your diet.

Your Food Choices Are Not Healthy Enough

Even if you are eating according to the keto diet or any other dietary style while you are intermittently fasting, it is not uncommon to find yourself eating the wrong food choices. Simply knowing what to eat and what to avoid is not enough. You need to spend some time getting to understand what specific vitamins and minerals you need to thrive. That way, you can eat a diet that is rich in these specific nutrients. Then, you can trust that your body has everything that it needs to thrive on your diet.

Even though intermittent fasting does not technically outline what you should and should not eat, it is not a one-size-fits-all diet that can help you lose weight while eating anything you want. In other words, excessive amounts of junk foods will still have a negative impact on you, even if you're eating during the right windows.

It is important that you choose a diet that is going to help you maintain everything you need to function optimally. Ideally, you should combine intermittent fasting with another diet such as the keto diet, the Mediterranean diet, or any other diet that supports you in eating healthfully. Following the guidelines of these healthier diets ensures that you are incorporating the proper nutrients into your diet so that you can stay healthy.

Eating the right nutrients is essential as it will support your body in healthy hormonal balances and bodily functions. This is how you can keep your organs functioning effectively so that everything works the way it should. As a result, you end up feeling healthier and experiencing greater benefits from your diet. It is imperative that you focus on this if you want to have success with your intermittent fasting diet.

You Are Not Drinking Enough Fluids

Many people do not realize how much hydration their foods actually give them on a day-to-day basis. Food like fruit and vegetables are filled with hydration that supports your body in healthily functions. If you are not eating much, then you can guarantee that you are not getting as much hydration as you actually need to. This means that you need to focus on increasing your hydration levels.

When you are dehydrated you can experience many unwanted symptoms that can make intermittent fasting a challenge. Increased headaches, muscle cramping and increased hunger are all side effects of dehydration. A great way to combat dehydration is to make sure that you keep water nearby and sip it often. At least once every 15 minutes to half an hour you should have a good drink of water. This will ensure that you are getting plenty of fresh water into your system.

Other ways that you can maintain your hydration levels include drinking low-calorie sports drinks, bone broth, tea and coffee. Essentially, drinking low-calorie drinks throughout the course of the entire day can be extremely helpful in supporting your health. Make sure that you do not exceed your fasting calorie maximum, however, or you will stop gaining the benefits of fasting. As well, water should always be your first choice above any other drinks to maintain your hydration. However, including some of the others from time to time can support you and keep things interesting so that you can stay hydrated, but not bored.

If you begin to experience any symptoms of dehydration, make sure that you immediately begin increasing the amount of water that you are drinking. Dehydration can lead to far more serious side effects beyond headaches and muscle cramps if you are not careful. If you find that you are prone to not drinking enough water on a daily basis, consider setting a reminder on your phone that keeps you drinking plenty throughout the day.

The best way to tell that you are staying hydrated enough is to pay attention to how frequently you are peeing. If you are staying in a healthy range of hydration, you should be peeing at least once every single hour. If you aren't, this means that you need to be drinking more water, even if you aren't experiencing any side effects of dehydration. Typically, if you have already begun experiencing side effects, then you have waited too long. You want to maintain healthy hydration without waiting for symptoms like headaches and muscle aches to inform you that it is time to start drinking more. This ensures that your body stays happy and healthy and that you are not causing unnecessary suffering or stress to your body throughout the day.

You Are Giving Up Too Quickly

A lot of people assume that eating the intermittent fasting diet means that they will see the benefits of their eating habits immediately. This is not the case. While intermittent fasting does typically offer great results fairly quickly, it does take some time for these results to begin appearing. The exact amount of time depends on many factors. How long it has taken you to transition, what and how you are eating during eating windows and how much activity you are getting throughout the day all contribute to your results.

You might feel compelled to quickly give up if you do not begin noticing your desired results right away, but trust that this is not going to help you. Some people require several weeks before they really begin seeing the benefits of their dieting. This does not mean that it is not working, it simply means that it has taken them some time to find the right balance so that they can gain their desired results and stay healthy.

If you are feeling like throwing in the towel, first take a few minutes to consider what you are doing and how it may be negatively impacting your results. A great way to do this is to try using your food diary once again. For a few days, track how you are eating in accordance with the intermittent fasting diet and what it is doing for you. Get a clear idea of how much you are eating, what you are eating and when you are eating it. Also, track the amount of physical activity that you are doing on a daily basis.

Through tracking your food intake and exercise levels, you might find that you are not experiencing the results you desire because you are eating too much or not enough in comparison to the amount of energy you are spending each day. Then, you can easily work towards adjusting your diet to find a balance that supports you in getting everything you need and also seeing the results that you desire.

In most cases, intermittent fasting diets are not working because they are not being used right for the individual person. Although the general requirements are somewhat the same, each of us has unique needs based on our lifestyles and our unique makeup. If you are willing to invest time in finding the right balance for yourself, then you can guarantee that you can overcome this and experience great results from your fasting.

You Are Getting Too Intense or Pushing It

If you are really focused on achieving your desired results, you might feel compelled to push your diet further than what is reasonable for you. For example, attempting to take on too intense of a fasting cycle or trying to do more than your body can reasonably handle. It is not uncommon for people to try and push themselves beyond reasonable measures to achieve their desired results. Unfortunately, this rarely results in them achieving what they actually set out to achieve. It can also have severe consequences.

At the end of the day, listening to your body and paying attention to exactly what it needs is important. You need to be taking care of yourself through proper nutrition and proper exercise levels. You also need to balance these two in a way that serves your body, rather than in a way that leads to you feeling sick and unwell. If you push your body too far, the negative consequences can be severe and long-lasting. In some cases, they may even be life-threatening.

In some cases, pushing your body to a certain extent is necessary. For example, if you are seeking to build more muscle, then you want to push yourself to work out enough that your workouts are actually effective. However, if you are pushing yourself to the point that you are beginning to experience negative side effects from your diet, you need to drawback. While certain amounts of side effects are fairly normal early on, experiencing intense side effects, having side effects that don't go away or having them return, is not good. You want to work towards maintaining and minimizing your side effects, not constantly living alongside them. After all, what is the point of adjusting your diet and lifestyle to serve your health if you are not actually feeling healthy while you do it?

Make sure that you check in with yourself on a daily basis to see to it that your physical needs are being met. That way, if anything begins to feel excessive or any symptoms begin to increase, you can focus on minimizing or eliminating them right away. Paying close attention to your needs and looking at your goals long-term rather than trying to reach them immediately is the best way to ensure that you reach your health goals without actually compromising your health while attempting to do so. In the end, you will feel much better about doing it this way.

How to Deal with Bad Days with IF

We all know in the 21st century that well-being starts with healthy eating habits. Then why is it so difficult to stick to a balanced diet? The grocery store's aisles, posters on the doctor's offices and even some TV advertisements use vivid colors and bold lettering to advertise healthy living. Women over 50 years are especially advised to watch what they eat as it is easier for them to gain weight than lose it.

The issue is not because people don't want to change their eating habits; it's that they don't even know how to do it. They get on board a new weight-loss plan, which they soon discard as such diets are often unsustainable when compared with regular lifestyles.

That's not the best way to go for a balanced lifestyle. Instead, you want to make a meaningful, permanent improvement, but you have to make sure you are doing it right. The guide below will help and show you how to stick to healthy eating habits. By setting realistic expectations and being persistent, you will find that good eating patterns are now well within your grasp even though they were impossible in the past. Each diet and weight-loss plan have their benefits and drawbacks, so you have to prepare your mind for it if you want to succeed.

The hardest factor in weight loss is changing your attitude about how to lose weight.

Many people attempt to lose weight with the worst imaginable mental state. They bolt into diets and workout programs out of personal deprecation, all the while squeezing their "trouble" spots, branding themselves "fat" and feeling entirely less than that. They get distracted with results, rely on fast solutions and lose sight of what good health is all about.

This kind of thought can be harmful. Instead of concentrating on the benefits that can come from weight loss - such as improved wellbeing, healthier life, greater satisfaction of daily lives and the avoidance of diabetes and cardiac disease - these people focus on their pessimistic feelings. Eventually, poor thinking leads to disappointment.

Changing your mentality about weight loss goes beyond feeling good; it's about the outcome. A study at the University of Syracuse indicates that the unhappier women are with their bodies, the more likely they are to skip exercise. And just focusing on the fact that you're overweight is forecasting a potential weight gain, according to studies reported in the International Journal of Obesity in 2015.

Although psychologists emphasize that your actions are determined by how you view yourself and your core personality (seeing yourself as being overweight or undesirable makes you behave accordingly), genetics may also play a role. A study published in Psychosomatic Medicine journal also suggested that cortisol, the stress hormone, is secreted by the adrenal glands every time you get yourself down or think about your weight, which further causes weight gain.

It All Starts with Your Mindset

The problem with a lot of trendy diets is that they don't want you to think differently. They tell you to make a drastic adjustment to your eating habits. This is not healthy. If you are actively trying to change your eating habits, then first you have to fix your way of thinking about food.

Many people who are struggling to eat healthily have what researchers term a "closed mentality." These people believe that nothing can ever change, and they take this belief with them in beginning a new weight loss plan. They think that their health issues are simply the effects of poor biology, or that the embarrassment of solving the problem would reverse any improvements.

For certain people with a fixed mentality, long before it begins, a change of diet is futile. In reality, many would prefer to stay obese because it feels safer and less stressful than attempting to make a change in lifestyle.

Unfortunately, anyone who wants to move to a healthier lifestyle without changing their attitude first will soon get discouraged. That's because the journey to a healthy lifestyle doesn't happen overnight. There are no magic foods, no matter what the magazine said or what some star did to shed baby weight or to dress for a new role. If you are someone with a fixed mindset starting a weight loss diet, you'll undoubtedly come to think the plan failed when you don't see any significant difference, reinforcing your original fears. The diet's failure will only make it harder for you to begin a new journey to eating healthy. There is another mindset that Psychologists refer to as a "growth mindset." While the fixed mindset believes little else can be changed, the growth mindset thinks things are continually evolving.

People with a growth mindset don't design their thoughts to be negative. Instead, they understand that small mistakes are just part of improvement. They realize that risks are only a minor problem in achieving something big. Therefore, people with a growth mindset recognize that progress needs incremental steps in the right direction, rather than resigning themselves to the inevitable.

What kind of attitude do you have? If you have a fixed mindset, how do you make the necessary change?

One of the easiest ways to begin making a change is by collecting information about the process. I highly recommend that you maintain a journal. This is so when you see subtle improvements leading up to a significant transition, they don't get lost. Start by writing down your expectations and record whether or not you have successfully met them.

A growth mindset is not a crazy dreamer mindset when it comes to goals. When setting your targets, always make sure that they are fair. Keep note of how many balanced meals you consume, relative to how many might not be. Act to increase the number of nutritious meals you consume each week.

You've got to understand more than anything that your mindset may be what held you off. The good news is that you're well on your way to make a meaningful difference when you know that mindset is part of the problem!

Below are some steps you can take to change your mindset.

Adjust Your Priorities

The reason might be to lose weight, but that should not be the target. Instead, the objectives should be small, manageable stuff that you have full power to control. Have you consumed five fruit and veggie servings today? That's one goal achieved. What about 8 hours of sleep; have you got them in? If so, you can cross them off your list.

Gravitate To Positivity

It is vital to surround yourself with the good. Doing so offers you a relaxing, socially healthy environment to invest in yourself. Don't be afraid to ask for help or support.

Rethink Punishments and Rewards

Remember that making healthier decisions is a way to practice self-care. Food is not a reward, and workout is not a penalty. They are all necessary to take care of your body and to make you do the best you can. You deserve both.

Taking a few minutes at the start of your exercise or at the beginning of your day to calm down, and simply concentrate on breathing will help you set your goals, communicate with your body and even reduce the stress response of your body.

Find a quiet space wherever you are (even at work) and try this exercise to help you feel more relaxed and ready to tackle the rest of your day. Lie with your legs outstretched on your back and put one hand on your stomach and one on your shoulder. Breathe in for 4 seconds through your nose, stay for two, and exhale for six seconds through your lips. Repeat this process for 5-10 minutes, focusing on the sensation of your stomach rising and falling with each breath.

Identify "Troublesome Thoughts"

Identify the feelings that bring you problems and seek to prevent and change them. Let them stop intentionally by saying "no" out loud. It may sound silly, but that simple action breaks your chain of thought and helps you to introduce a new, safer one. The easiest way to do so is to count as many times as you like from one to 100 until your negative thoughts go away.

Don't Step On the Scale

Even though stepping on the scale to check on your progress is not bad, many people often associate it with negative thoughts. If you know the number on the scale will lead to negative and self-destructive thoughts, then you should avoid it. At least until you are in a place where the number on the scale doesn't affect your mental health.

Speak to Yourself as a Friend

When it comes to beauty and body image expectations, we're incredibly harsh on ourselves. We punish ourselves with the standard we set. This is a widespread problem for people today, especially women with advertisements and images of a specific body type. Building a positive body image is an excellent way to counteract this negative stream of images we are encouraged to compare ourselves to. Improving your body image can be hard, but it's certainly doable. Focus on your positive qualities, skills and talents. Focus on appreciating and respecting what your body can do. Say positive things to yourself every day. Avoid negative or berating self-talk. Admire the beauty of others, but avoid comparing yourself to anyone else. Handle yourself like this.

Forget About the Entire "Foods" Attitude

We've learned somewhere along the way to feel either proud or bad for any food choice we make. But in the end, it's just food, so you shouldn't feel bad for enjoying an occasional cookie. Permit yourself to have a piece of chocolate cake or a glass of wine sometimes.

Treating yourself to some comfort food is right for your mind and body. It is doing it every day that sabotages weight loss. During a more or less strict diet, having a day in a week to get away from it is the key to success, the guarantee for motivation and does not undermine the goal of losing weight.

Focus On the Attainable

If you've never been to a gym before, your goal on day one shouldn't be to do 30 minutes on the elliptical. Going for a 30-minute walk might be a better goal. If you want to cook more, but have little familiarity with healthier cooking, don't bank on creating new nutritious recipes every night after work. Instead, consider using a subscription service such as Blue Apron or HelloFresh, where pre-portioned recipes and ingredients are delivered to your doorstep, helping you get to know different components, make new meals and develop your cooking skills.

Envision a Better Life

What will life be like if you put good habits in place? Will you be more comfortable in your clothes? Will it give you more energy? Will you sleep better? Will you laugh more? Will you be happier? Will you be a better wife or mum? Attempt to get as thorough and realistic as possible. How will your life change if you changed your lifestyle?

Take time to visualize a better life in the beginning and throughout your weight loss plan. Changing your habits is hard, so why bother if it doesn't bring you something new and better. Imagine a better life that will start giving you something to look forward to as well as work towards. See what you want, get a picture of it in your mind. Vision is going to direct your life.

The "Law of Thinking" of Bob Proctor, states: "The Law of Thinking dictates that we can only attract what we think. By changing your conscious thought pattern, which is your ruling state, you will allow yourself to change the result to what you want effectively. How far a person can go or how great the success a person can have depends on the thinking." "Visualization is where everything starts."

Believe You Are in Control

You must realize you control your life. You have to take responsibility for your actions to excel in losing weight and other goals; you have to trust that you are in charge. If you put your future in other people's hands, you will never be able to move on. Of course, there are always circumstances out of our control, but your type of reaction is up to you.

While taking control of your life is empowering, it's also frightening because if you don't achieve your goal, you have no one to blame but yourself. "No one has control over your life, but you."

Get to Learn How to Cope

Many of your problems with weight loss are from your physiological reactions to stress. Most times, you crave spaghetti or candy when you have a bad day. Or you order a pizza because there was nothing to cook for dinner. Or give up on losing weight when work gets busy, or when you get to some other stressful season of life.

When you want to lose weight, life doesn't just continue effortlessly without stress. Sadly, life will never be secure and there will always be a pain. Consequently, if you fall off track each time, life does not go your way, then it is time you learn new coping strategies. The goal is to maintain a healthy lifestyle and lose weight, no matter the obstacles life throws our way.

If the way you cope with stress keeps you from putting new behaviors in place or maintaining them, you might want to talk to a therapist or counselor. A therapist or psychologist will help you develop healthier coping skills and work through stress. This will help you free up space in your brain to focus on that better life. Having excellent optimistic coping skills is necessary for growth and surviving, not just for weight loss. Life is unpredictable and will not always go according to plan. Either you can get better or get bitter.

"The secret of success is learning how to use pain and pleasure instead of having pain and pleasure use you. If you do that, you're in control of your life. If you don't, life controls you." - Tony Robbins.

Eliminate the Clutter and the Chaos

What do clutter and chaos have to do with weight loss? It's tough to picture a happier future when you are surrounded by confusion and noise. Clutter and confusion build hot zones, and when attempting to escape hot zones, it's challenging to develop new patterns and behaviors. Hot zones are moments when you feel stressed, overwhelmed and the decisions you make are more about surviving the moment than on long-term goals.

Concentrate On Solutions and Not Explanations

A proactive approach that has been effective in the weight loss process is relying on options instead of excuses. You may be using excuses because you're scared of failing. So you say something like, "I can't get to the gym at that time" or "I 'm sick" or "That exercise never worked for me" instead of falling into an exercise routine. It offers you the freedom to either give up or not try at all. Failure, however, is part of the process. Failure is good. And instead of making yourself give up, grant yourself the approval to lose. To succeed, you have to be okay with failure, not just at losing weight but in life in general.

Say Thank You

It's so crucial to express gratitude for everything life offers us. Feeling thankful makes us humble and appreciative of the struggles we have made to accomplish goals. It says thank you to the universe and recognizes all of your efforts.

If you're trying to change habits or work past hard times, try to take time every day and talk about 1-3 things for which you're grateful, like genuine thanks. Talk of the lessons learned and how, because of that, you will get stronger. Life is short or long, and being thankful will help you appreciate everything that you have, rather than focusing on the negative. Your life will change just by thinking more positively.

"Gratitude is a powerful process for shifting your energy and bringing more of what you want into your life. Be grateful for what you already have, and you will attract more good things." - Bob Proctor.

Talk with Your Doctor

Any improvement in lifestyle should be made with the feedback from your doctor. There will be many blogs selling the perfect diet. However, the fact is that our bodies are different, and the needs of everyone are different. Make sure to talk to a professional who is knowledgeable of your medical history to get the best results in your attempt to begin a healthy lifestyle. They can thus help you in making choices that are right for you. Your doctor may recommend a healthy heart diet if you have high cholesterol. Or, they might recommend a higher calorie intake if you are incredibly active in supporting your exercise. Regardless, you should never change your eating habits without consulting your primary care physician first.

Other Changes in Lifestyle Which Promote Healthy Eating

Here are some further tips for changing your eating patterns with that in mind:

Get Enough Sleep

An essential part of any good lifestyle is the proper amount of sleep. You cannot realize that, but having only 30 minutes less sleep than your body demands will reduce your energy and motivation to exercise. Simultaneously, having too much sleep is also correlated with a slower metabolism, as it reduces the number of calories you consume in a day. So, find a happy medium and commit to it, just like the recommended seven to nine hours. When you are full of functional strength, you will quickly find committing to a healthy lifestyle is simpler.

Don't Over-Rely On Exercise

Ancient wisdom said the more you exercise, the more you can eat. This may not necessarily be true. Studies have shown that what you eat affects health much more than how much you exercise. And while you want to make sure you eat enough to help your workout routine, frequent workouts don't offer your carte blanche to eat anything you want. However, that just doesn't mean the workout is not essential either. A healthy, active lifestyle that includes at least one hour of exercise each day is the best way to ensure the improvements in your lifestyle will have the kinds of effects you are searching for.

How You Can Tell Change Is Happening

Although you should be pursuing a change in lifestyle with the awareness that real-lasting transition takes time, however, you want to see results at some stage. So, how can you say the change that you've worked so hard for is happening?

Remember what mindset is all about? Take some time after a month or two of real commitment to change and test your attitude again. What's different in that? Furthermore, you should not feel guilty about it when you engage in it. If you feel like a failure eating a cookie or a slice of pie, you're approaching it with the wrong attitude. If you use the right healthy eating mindset, when you treat yourself to a bowl of ice cream after eating well all week, you will not feel like a failure.

Finally, if your attitude has changed, you shouldn't feel so compelled to overeat. You should eat an adequate amount when you are hungry, just enough to make you feel full. When you feel full, you should stop. You're not supposed to feel pressure to clean your plate, finish the box, or have dessert just because it's there.

Look back at the first things you wrote in your journal of change when you started this journey. Compare those things today with the way you talk about health and life. Don't be so worried about which notch you use in your belt. Then look at the effect on your health in the long run.

A balanced lifestyle is an essential aspect of a long and happy life, complete with fitness, cooking well and having enough time to relax. It's not a transition that we need to make because we look pretty on the sand. It's the kind of shift in mindset that can make you happy, more fulfilled and healthy throughout your life.

It is also essential that beneficial changes in lifestyle are the sort that will last. Don't get distracted from making progress that lasts a lifetime. Fast improvements would only prevent you from trying to make more potential changes.

"Results are a direct reflection of your thoughts, your beliefs, your habits: your mindset."

Change your mindset, and you'll be happier and healthier than you ever knew. And this all leads to something else, a change in your eating habits.

Because you can only eat during a certain window of time, you'll want to make the most of it. By feeding your body healthy, nutritious and delicious foods, you won't want to go back to eating junk. Sure, you can "treat" yourself occasionally, but I promise you this: after a while on intermittent fasting, once your body gets used to eating a healthier diet, you won't want those treats.

One more thing you need to understand: this won't happen overnight. You have to work at changing both your mindset and your habits, so be patient and give yourself time.

Best Home Exercise During Your IF

Yet, many may wonder if it's safe to exercise during an intermittent fast. With the body depleted of nutrients during a fast after all, would it be wise to put it through any more strain than it's already under? According to the data, exercising while undergoing a fast has a direct effect on metabolism and the body's level of insulin. Both are activated with one going up and the other going down as the body recalibrates and begins to burn fat rather than carbs. Engaging in the right kind of workout will help to speed up this process even more. Having that said, here are some exercises to give your intermittent fast a major boost.

Weightlifting

If you are a weightlifter or interested in becoming one, I have some good news for you. Lifting weights does not interfere with your fast! In fact, lifting weights during a fast can prove quite beneficial. The very style of intermittent fasting is designed to prevent muscle loss during fasting periods, but having that said, a little weightlifting will help to shield your body from muscle loss even more. Because the truth is, we all lose muscle as we age and if we don't work at maintaining it through muscle lifting, we just might find that our muscle mass is declining significantly through the years. Even more beneficial for those wishing to lose weight, lifting weights during an intermittent fast also quickens the pace of fat burn even more. Just think about it; during a fast, your body has already switched to burning fat for its fuel, so when you grunt, struggle and strain to lift those weights, guess what your body's tapping into for energy? All that fat you want to get rid of! Do I dare say: this is a win-win situation? It most certainly is!

Pushups

One of the most traditional exercises you could ever even consider would be that of the classic pushup. Pushups have been around forever and there is a reason for that, they are highly effective. By making use of gravity and your own body weight, the push-up gets the heart going while the muscles do overtime to push the body up off the floor by virtue of arm strength alone. These exercises, if done moderately - say no more than 20 to 30 pushups during a fast - can be highly effective in boosting your metabolism to the max, allowing an even more rapid depletion of the body's fat stores. This is some good news that you could most certainly use!

Running/Treadmill

There is really nothing better to get the body's metabolic cylinders running than a good run. As soon as your feet hit the pavement (or the treadmill), your heart rate increases and the blood starts to much more vigorously pump through your body. With your bodily processes instantly speeding up like this, it's really no wonder that your metabolism might speed up as well. And this is precisely the case when you engage in this type of exercise during a fast. But having that said, just keep in mind that you have to be careful not to overdo it. And in order to ensure that you have the best experience, it is recommended that you only run during the first few hours of your fast. That way, your body still has plenty of additional resources left over from the last meal you had before your fast began. If for example, you begin your fast at 10 pm on a Thursday night, you should be good to run around the block at 7 am Friday morning without any trouble. It is not advisable, however, to overexert yourself at the very end of your fast. Although most could probably handle it, just to be on the safe side, you should keep your running hours locked into the first few hours of your fast. Every step you take causes hormones to alert your metabolic engines that you are up and quite literally *running*.

Squats

This is another great exercise that seems absolutely made for intermittent fasting. Squats focus on your glutes, quads and other muscles like there is no tomorrow! This exercise keeps you going and keeps you strong! As you might imagine, squats consist of the participant bending their knees and squatting down toward the ground as if they are sitting on a chair. This bending motion gets the blood flowing to the thighs and begins rapidly burning fat deposits. If you need to target fat in the legs, in particular, you might want to give this exercise a try.

But how do you squat? Correct posture is essential both to benefit from the toning effects of the exercise and to avoid incurring tears or painful contractures. So the squat mimics the act of sitting, but without the chair. Although, the first few times, perhaps it would be useful to use a chair, obviously without being able to lean on it, merely keeping it as a reference point.

To begin, start by standing up straight, then place your feet apart and look straight in front of you. Lower your body as if you are about to sit on a chair. Lower yourself and stop only when your thighs are parallel to the floor. With your upper body leaning slightly forward, rise slowly into a standing position. Repeat for ten or more times.

Dips

Why yes, we would be remiss if we did not mention dips! And no, I'm not talking about the stuff you dip your chips in at the football game, I'm talking about high intensity, fat-burning exercise that will burn fat, boost your metabolism and make sure your upper body stays nice and strong. These exercises are just about perfect for intermittent fasting as they get the blood flowing without making you too tired in the process.

Reverse Lunge

This exercise may look easy at first glance but don't be fooled. Reverse lunges are a high-intensity workout that gets your metabolism going. And when done during a fast, it really kicks things into high gear. They are also good for getting your legs in tip-top shape which is beneficial for just about every other aerobic exercise you could do. For a lunge, stand with your feet only a few inches apart and your eyes staring straight ahead. Step forward with just a leg while lowering your hips slowly towards the ground with your knees bent. The knees of your forward leg should be in line with your ankle instead of just jutting it out. You can keep your arms at your sides, or you can raise them above your head. Stay in the lunge position for a beat before going back to standing. Repeat for a few minutes by alternating your legs.

Burpee

No, a burpee isn't what happens when you eat too many hot peppers. A bad joke maybe, but in all seriousness, there are many out there who are confused with what a burpee is and what it is not. The Burpee is a classic hybrid-styled exercise that makes full use of cardio as well as resistance exercises, in order to maximize your metabolism. These exercises are pretty intensive, so if you are engaged in a less-than-500-calorie fast day, you might want to actually have a low-calorie snack or other healthy option. Good choices for nutrition before this workout would be perhaps just a hard-boiled egg, a salad, or maybe even a bowl of chicken broth. Either way, these workouts are sure to get your body running on all cylinders during your intermittent fast.

Planks

Planks are a fairly common yet highly efficient exercise that can be done at home, at the gym, or just about any place you may be at the time. This exercise is also quite nuanced and flexible when it comes to adjusting the intensity and the area of focus. Planks tend to build up quite a bit of endurance too, which is most certainly good for someone who is undergoing a fast. It is best to engage in this exercise during the first few hours of your fast, but they can be done periodically throughout the rest of the fasting day as well.

Yoga

Yoga is good for everyone: men, women and children, but it is especially excellent for all women. We, women, have precise needs, problems and stages of life. Just think for a moment about how much a woman's attitude and physical health are affected by hormones, which control the menstrual cycle, pregnancy and menopause. Yoga balances these hormones efficiently and effectively during the many stages of life.

Yoga, however, is not only for the changes in the body to which women are subjected, but also serves to balance emotions, to reduce the impact of diseases such as breast cancer and osteoporosis and for the female need to have a way to live comfortable and relaxed, following the spiritual attitude.

Yoga is one of the most straightforward workouts you can do. No matter your abilities and needs, there are many yoga styles designed to meet your needs. Maybe you want to stretch your body or relax, or perhaps you want to calm down, yoga can help you achieve all these.

All you need is a yoga mat, or you can use your home carpet if it's comfortable and soft. You can get some props like blocks and straps, but you can replace them with other objects. You can use rolls of paper towels or a stack of books instead as a yoga block for extra lift during poses. You can use an old pair of leggings or tights as straps and a pillow or folded blanket as a bolster.

In the most common yoga exercises, you work simultaneously on strength, balance and stretching. Thanks to the different types of positions practiced, you get these benefits:

- Greater oxygenation of internal organs and tissues, therefore a detox action
- Posture improvement, especially in the case of "alignment focused" practices
- Flexibility and ease of movement

- Muscle toning
- Improved blood circulation
- Breath control and regularization
- Improvement of blood pressure
- Stabilization of blood sugar
- Increase in bone mass
- Improvement of digestive problems
- Stimulation of the parasympathetic nervous system

Walking the Stairs

Walking up and down the stairs allows you to improve the health of your heart and lungs, has a low impact on the joint, and is useful for developing speed, power and agility.

It is an exercise at no cost, which does not require technical clothing or special equipment. If you don't have stairs at home or in a condominium, you can use those of urban public areas, in any case, even a simple step or a small stool can come to the rescue wherever you are. To spice things up, you can do an aerobic step exercise. Try to go up and down from the first step to the landing.

You can train at different degrees of intensity depending on your physical condition. This type of training leads the lower body muscles (thighs, buttocks and calves) to work hard anyway, as they have to repeatedly lift the upper part of the person in a vertical movement that goes against the force of gravity.

When you go up and down the stairs, with a certain intensity, you burn a high amount of fat more than running and fast walking. This simple activity can also help strengthen the muscles that stabilize the knees, ligaments and cartilages; in this regard, stairs are often included in rehabilitation activities. It also helps to normalize blood pressure levels and heart health in general. It is an excellent exercise to improve balance, strength, endurance and sculpt and slim the muscles of the lower body.

FAQ

Fasting can be difficult at times and we know it! There are certain concerns that every beginner gets after opting for intermittent fasting. The following frequently asked questions can help resolve basic queries about fasting and its effects on health.

#1: What Can I Eat or Drink During Fasting?

As we said earlier, to reap the full benefits that intermittent fasting can provide, you simply shouldn't eat or drink anything that has calories.

On the other hand, we also argue that small amounts of good fats will not hinder your goals if you are only looking to control your insulin.

And finally, we also say that some authors defend the idea that eating very few calories (up to 50 kcal) would not break your fast, regardless of the source of those calories.

Even so, we know that some people prefer a summary list of foods to help them get started.

This practical list helps to remember which foods and drinks can or cannot be consumed during the fast window, without necessarily "breaking your fast" or ending all its benefits.

For this reason, we have put down a short non-exhaustive list of foods that can be eaten without disturbing your fast.

#2: What About Sweetened Foods But No Calories? Like Coffee with Stevia, Erythritol or Sucralose, and Even Zero Soda?

By now, you have understood that the idea of intermittent fasting is not to consume food, so as not to ingest calories, or to raise insulin.

So, using non-caloric sweeteners should be allowed, right?

Calm down. This issue is more complex than it may seem at first.

First, I strongly recommend that you understand the differences between the different types of low-carb sweeteners.

But, as we explained, even if we consider only sweeteners that do not raise insulin (as is the case with stevia, or even erythritol, for example), we still have an important question.

Although this relationship is speculative - that is, unproven - there are possibly several potential mechanisms through which the use of sweeteners can interfere with metabolism.

And that even includes interactions with sweet taste receptors, which would stimulate other metabolic adaptations.

Certainly, more research is needed, but in our opinion, this is yet another sign that it can be smart not to abuse sweeteners.

And in our personal opinion, one thing is certain: the daily consumption of sweeteners is not ideal for your health, even though it may not hinder weight loss or break your fast.

Especially in the case of artificial sweeteners, and even more so in the case of zero soft drinks.

#3: Who Can Do Intermittent Fasting?

An important question that people often have when we talk about fasting and its benefits is precisely who can and cannot fast (practice it).

The direct answer is that the practice of intermittent fasting is suitable for healthy adults.

It is even easier to speak who should not start fasting without first talking to their trusted doctor.

#4: Does Fasting Slow Metabolism?

If you are paying attention to this text, you should already intuitively know the answer to that question.

No, intermittent fasting does not slow down metabolism.

The keyword in this sentence is "intermittent."

For it is clear that to spend very long periods (several and several days) without eating will imply a metabolic adaptation (that is, a slowing down of the metabolism).

Just as a very long and/or severe caloric restriction will also have the same effect.

This is because our body seeks to survive above all else.

So, if you go without eating for several days, your body will seek to preserve energy.

However, on short fasts, our metabolism tends to increase.

In this case, one study found a 3.6% increase in metabolism on short fasts - and another study found that metabolism increased 10% during fasting.

This makes evolutionary sense: if our body seeks to feed, it needs to stimulate us, and not deprive us of the energy we have - so that we can hunt/collect food and thus obtain energy.

This is probably mediated by hormonal changes that occur during fasting, such as increased adrenaline.

#5: Intermittent Fasting Causes Loss of Muscle Mass (Lean Mass)?

Another very common question is regarding the conservation of muscle mass when we practice fasting.

This question arises mainly because we always hear around (especially repeated as a mantra in gyms), that if you didn't eat every three hours, your body would start to burn muscles to provide you with energy.

Unfortunately, this is a very common myth, and we just have no idea where it came from.

If you read the question about "eating every 3 hours" that we answered above, then you understand that you don't have to eat every 3 hours to conserve your muscle mass.

On the other hand, you may be wondering if taking longer periods without eating (16, 24, 48 hours, or more) would damage your lean mass.

But you can rest easy: during the fasting window, you will not break muscles as a form of energy.

In fact, your muscles can even serve as an energy source, but you have other reserves that are much easier for your body to use, such as fat in your belly and elsewhere, and glycogen.

Remembering that glycogen is our energy reserve in the form of carbohydrates, which is stored both in the liver and in the muscles, between the muscle cells.

#6: Can I Exercise During Fasting?

Another very common question concerns fasting and physical exercise.

The most common questions are:

1. Can I train while fasting?
2. Can I not eat anything after training?
3. Can I train while fasting and continue to fast afterward?

Briefly, the answer to these questions and their variations is: you can do whatever you want.

You can train on a fast if you feel good, for example.

At the same time that there are people who are not feeling well, in which case they probably shouldn't be training fasting.

Of course, if you're on a high-carb, especially refined diet, eating every three hours; for a low-carb diet and still, start fasting and training hard, so it's normal that you don't feel well.

You need to give your body time to adapt to all these changes.

However, we believe that most people can, indeed, train while fasting after some time of adaptation, if they want to do so.

That is, there is nothing special about being fasting that prevents you from training.

You can even practice fasting and then fast for a few more hours until your lunch.

As we mentioned in the case of lean gains fasting, you don't necessarily need to have your first meal right before or right after your workout.

#7: Which Supplements Do Not Break Intermittent Fasting?

Now that you know you can train on an empty stomach, without eating anything before and nothing afterward, maybe your next question is precisely related to supplements.

As we have said before, theoretically, fasting is a period when you should not eat anything.

However, there are exceptions, as in the case of insulin fasting.

So it is natural that doubts related to supplements arise as well.

Especially because there are supplements that do not really break the fast, because they do not contain calories.

#8: Can I Take Bone Broth?

First of all: what is bone broth and why would anyone be interested in taking it?

In short, bone broth is the drink obtained by boiling the bones and connective tissue of different types of animals.

It is rich in vitamins, minerals, collagen and other nutrients.

And it is precisely because the bone broth is rich in nutrients that it becomes interesting for longer fasts. Because it has the ability to replace nutrients (vitamins and minerals) lost during the fasting window.

After all, you are frequently eliminating water and minerals during this period through urine and perspiration.

#9: What to Say When Someone Criticizes Your Fasting?

The truth is that, even with all the support that science gives to this practice, fasting is still a controversial topic for most people. As strange as it may be that we live in a society in which we skip meals occasionally and eat real food are controversial.

So don't be alarmed if you receive unwanted criticism or comments from friends and family.

Breakfast Recipes

Mexican Egg & Tortilla Skillet
Time: 25 Mins, Serves: 4, Skill: Easy

Ingredients
- Unsalted tortilla chips (6 oz.)
- Butter (2 tbsp)
- Low salt ketchup (1/4 cup)
- Chili powder (1 tsp)
- Green onions (2), sliced thin
- Eggs (8)

Instructions
- Whisk the eggs together in a mixing bowl until well combined.
- Combine the ketchup, cabbage, and chili powder with the egg mixture. Blend until it's almost completely smooth.
- In a pan, melt the butter, then add the tortilla chips and cook over medium heat until heated through.
- Stir in the egg mixture to the tortillas, and scramble until you reach the desired consistency. Serve right away on warm plates.

40-Second Omelet
Time: 25 Mins, Serves: 1, Skill: Easy

Ingredients
- Eggs (2)
- Water (2 tbsp)
- Filling (vegetables, meat, seafood) (1/2 cup)
- Unsalted butter (1 tbsp)

Instructions
- Combine the eggs and water in a mixing bowl and whisk until smooth.
- Melt the butter in a 10" omelet pan/frypan until a water drop sizzles.
- Pour the egg mixture into the pan, quickly spreading it out on the sides, and using an inverted pancake turner, carefully push cooked portions from the edges to the center, allowing uncooked portions to come into contact with the heated pan's surface. Tilt and move the pan as desired.
- If necessary, fill the omelet with 1/2 cup beef, vegetables, or seafood filling, placing the filling on the left side if you're right-handed and on the right side if you're left-handed.
- Invert the bottom half of the omelet onto a plate using the pancake turner.

Stuffed Breakfast Biscuits
Time: 40 Mins, Serves: 4, Skill: Easy

Ingredients
- Milk (3/4cup)
- Eggs (4)
- Reduced-sodium bacon (8 0z.)
- Cheddar cheese (1 cup), shredded
- Scallions (1/4 cup), thinly sliced
- Flour (2 cups)
- Sugar (or honey) (1 tbsp)
- Baking soda (1/2 tsp)
- Lemon juice (1 tbsp)
- Softened unsalted butter (8 tbsp)

Instructions
- Preheat oven to 425ºF.
- Crisp up the bacon in a pan.
- Place the four ingredients in a mixing bowl and set aside. (Eggs, bacon, cheese, and scallions.)

The dough should be made as follows:

- Combine all of the dry ingredients in a big mixing cup.
- Break the unsalted butter into small pea-sized pieces with a fork or pastry knife.
- Make a "well" in the center of the dough and knead in the milk and lemon juice.
- Lightly flour the bottom and sides of muffin tins or line them with parchment paper.

- Fill muffin tins with a quarter-cup of the mixture.
- Bake for 10 minutes, or until golden brown.

Cheesesteak Quiche
Time: 50 Mins, Serves: 6, Skill: Easy

Ingredients
- Eggs, beaten (5)
- Cream (1 cup)
- Cooked prepared piecrust (1" x 9")
- Black pepper (1/2 tsp)
- Coarsely chopped Sirloin steak meat (1/2 lb.)
- Onions (1 cup), diced
- Canola oil (2 tbsp)
- Shredded pepper jack cheese (1/2 cup)

Instructions
- Cut the sliced sirloin into coarse pieces.
- Brown the sliced steak and onions in a sauté pan with the oil, then set aside to cool for 10 minutes before folding in the cheese and letting it rest.
- Whisk the eggs, cream, and black pepper in a large mixing cup until thoroughly combined.
- Spread the steak and cheese mixture on the bottom of the par-cooked piecrust, then top with the egg mixture and bake at 350°F for 30 minutes.
- Cover the cheesesteak quiche with foil and turn off the oven for 10 minutes before serving.

Homemade Muesli
Time: 55 Mins, Serves: 5, Skill: Medium

Ingredients
- Coconut (unsweetened) (1/3 cup), shredded
- Shelled pumpkin seeds (3/4 cup)
- Dried cranberries (3/4 cup)
- Raisins (1/2 cup)
- Apples, dried (1 cup), finely chopped
- Dried apricots (1/2 cup), finely chopped
- Chia seeds (1/4 cup)
- Rolled oats (1 3/4 cups)

- Honey (1 1/2 tbsp)

Instructions
- In a big mixing cup, combine the dried apples and apricots.
- All of the ingredients can be mixed, including chia seeds, cranberries, pumpkin seeds, raisins, coconut, and oats.
- Mix all in until it's almost smooth.
- Mix in the honey until the paste is only mildly lumpy (but not sticky).
- It goes well with almond milk, daily yogurt, and non-dairy yogurt.

Egg Sandwich
Time: 25 Mins, Serves: 4, Skill: Easy

Ingredients
- Egg (1)
- Water (1 tbsp)
- A pinch of salt
- A pinch of black pepper
- Cheddar cheese (1 slice)
- Wheat bread (2 slices)
- Basil leaves (3 meds)
- Olive oil (1/2 tbsp)
- Tomato (2 slices)

Instructions
- In a toaster or dry skillet, toast the bread and put it aside.
- Separate the basil leaves from the stems and position them in a separate bowl.
- Heat some olive oil in a small skillet over medium heat.
- After scrambling the eggs with water, season them with pepper and salt.
- Pour it into the skillet and cook the omelet in one layer without folding halfway around, then flip to cook the other side.
- Layering the ingredients: cheese on the warm bread slice, then the egg, with the sides rolled under for bread size fitting, then slices of

tomatoes, basil leaves, then a second bread slice on top.

- When the sandwich is still tender, cut it diagonally in half and eat.

Southern Style Grits
Time: 55 Mins, Serves: 2, Skill: Medium

Ingredients
- Water (1 cup)
- Milk (1/3 cup)
- Salt (1/8 tsp)
- Butter (1 tbsp)
- Salt, to taste (optional)
- Stone-ground grits (1/3 cup)
- Pepper, to taste (opt)

Instructions
- In a shallow saucepan, combine the grits, milk, salt, water, and half of the butter.
- Bring them to a boil, then reduce to low heat and simmer for 30 to 40 minutes, stirring continuously to avoid sticking.
- Add the remaining butter and season with salt and pepper to taste, if necessary.

Cherry Overnight Oats
Time: 25 Mins, Serves: 1, Skill: Easy

Ingredients
- Almond milk (1/2 cup)
- Honey (2 tsp)
- Cinnamon (1/8 tsp)
- Old fashioned rolled oats (1/2 cup)
- Sweet cherries (1/2 cup), pitted and halved

Instructions
- In a mason jar, mix all ingredients and swirl to combine.
- Cover it and keep it refrigerated overnight.

Chili Wheat Treats
Time: 30 Mins, Serves: 2, Skill: Easy

Ingredients
- Dash cayenne pepper

- Garlic powder (1/2 tsp)
- Spoon-size shredded wheat (4 cups)
- Margarine (1/2 cup)
- Chili powder (1 tbsp)
- Ground cumin (1/2 tsp)

Instructions
- Before baking, preheat the oven to 300 °F.
- In a 10" x 15" baking pan, dissolve the margarine.
- Combine the herbs in a separate dish. Evenly distribute the wheat and toss to cover.
- Preheat oven to 350°F and bake for 15 minutes, or until crisp. Keep in a pan with a lid.

Burritos with Eggs and Mexican Sausage
Time: 25 Mins, Serves: 4, Skill: Easy

Ingredients
- Eggs, beaten (3)
- Flour tortillas (3)
- Chorizo (3 oz.)

Instructions
- In a skillet, fry the chorizo until it turns a dark brown color.
- Cook the eggs until they are cooked through.
- Fill the tortillas halfway with the filling, roll them to prevent the filling from leaking out, and fold the bottom edge in.

Parmesan Cheese Spread
Time: 4 hours 10 Mins, Serves: 4, Skill: Easy

Ingredients
- Garlic powder (1/4 tsp)
- Cream cheese (3-oz), 1 package
- Parmesan cheese (2 tbsps.), grated
- Margarine (4 tbsps.), softened
- Dry white wine (1 tbsp)
- Dash of marjoram
- Dash of thyme
- Parsley (1 tbsp), minced

Instructions

- Mix all of the ingredients together well in a big mixing tub. Refrigerate for at least 4 hours.
- Serve with unsalted crackers, Melba bread, or celery stuffing to round out the meal.

Cranberry Salad
Time: 17 Mins, Serves: 4, Skill: Easy

Ingredients

- 2 raspberry packages (3-oz)
- Jell-O
- Whole cranberry sauce (1 can), not jellied
- Celery (1 cup), chopped
- Apples (1 cup), chopped & peeled
- Unsalted nuts (1/2 cup)

Instructions

- Prepare Jell-O as directed on the box.
- Add the raspberry, apples, cranberry sauce, celery, and nuts while they are all cool and syrupy. Refrigerate until fully set.

Spiced Pineapple Appetizer
Time: 25 Mins, Serves: 4, Skill: Easy

Ingredients

- Sugar (3 tbsps.)
- Garlic powder (1/8 tsp)
- White wine vinegar (1/4 cup)
- Crushed red pepper (1/4 tsp)
- Lime juice (2 tbsps.)
- Dijon mustard (1/2 tsp)
- Chunks of pineapple (20-oz), drained

Instructions

- In a saucepan, whisk together the sugar, vinegar, Dijon mustard, lime juice, seasoning, and garlic powder.
- Bring to a boil. Reduce the heat to low and cook for 3 minutes with the lid on.
- Combine the vinegar mixture with the pineapple in a cup and combine well. Serve with toothpicks to keep it soft.

Strawberry Stuffing
Time: 45 Mins, Serves: 3, Skill: Easy

Ingredients

- Tart apples (1 cup), diced, peeled
- Strawberries (1/2 cup), diced
- Celery (1/4 cup), chopped
- Poultry seasoning (1/4 tsp)
- Apple juice (1/4 cup)
- Bread crumbs (3 cups)
- Unsalted Margarine (2 tbsps.), melted

Instructions

- Preheat the oven to 350 °F. In a mixing dish, combine all the ingredients, toss to mix thoroughly.
- Position it in a casserole dish that has been well greased. Bake for 30 minutes.

Crispy Fried Okra
Time: 35 Mins, Serves: 2, Skill: Easy

Ingredients

- 1 package frozen okra (16-oz), 1-inch segment
- Margarine (2 tbsp)
- Cornmeal (1/2 cup)
- Flour (1/2 cup)
- Beer/water (1 cup)
- Pepper (1/4 tsp)

Instructions

- Defrost the okra if frozen. In a mixing bowl, combine cornmeal, flour, and pepper. Break the margarine into the mixture until it becomes crumbly.
- After dipping the okra in water or cider, coat it in the cornmeal mixture.
- Place it on a baking sheet that has been greased. Preheat the oven to 350 °F and bake for 20 minutes, or until golden brown.
- Serve with toothpicks and low-sodium ketchup as a garnish.

Vegetable Recipes

Italian Eggplant Salad
Time: 25 Mins, Serves: 4, Skill: Easy

Ingredients
- Black pepper (1/4 tsp)
- Tomato (1 med), chopped
- Olive oil (3 tbsp)
- Eggplant (3 cups), cubed
- Onion (1 small), chopped
- White wine vinegar (2 tbsp)
- Garlic clove (1), chopped
- Oregano (1/2 tsp)

Instructions
- Put the eggplant in a pot of water that has been brought to a simmer.
- Bring the water to a boil and then reduce the heat.
- Cook for a further 10 minutes with the saucepan lid on.
- Drain the eggplants and place them in serving dishes with the onions and tomato.
- In a shallow dish, combine the garlic, oregano, vinegar, and black pepper.
- Combine the onions, tomato, and eggplant with the vinegar mixture.
- Drizzle a little oil over the eggplant mixture before serving.

Pineapple Coleslaw
Time: 1 hour 15 Mins, Serves: 3, Skill: Easy

Ingredients
- Pineapple (8 oz.), drained
- Cabbage (2 cups), shredded
- Miracle Whip (1/4 cup)
- Pepper, to taste
- Onion (1/4 cup), chopped

Instructions
- In a large mixing cup, combine the cabbage, whip, pineapple, pepper, and onion.
- Chill for 60 minutes before serving.

Roasted tomatillo salsa
Time: 45 Mins, Serves: 8, Skill: Medium

Ingredients
- Lime juice (1/4 cup)
- Cilantro (1 bunch)
- Water (1/4 cup)
- Tomatillos (17)
- Head garlic (1)
- Jalapenos (3)

Instructions
- Start by slicing the tomatillos.
- In a greased baking pan, mix the tomatillos, jalapenos, and garlic.
- To simmer in water, put them in the oven for 15 minutes.
- In a processor, puree the cooked tomatillo mixture with lime juice and cilantro until creamy.

Smoothie bowl
Time: 20 Mins, Serves: 1, Skill: Easy

Ingredients
- Blueberries (1 tbsp), fresh
- Unsweetened coconut (1 tbsp), shredded
- Protein powder (2 tbsp)
- Banana (1/2)
- Strawberries (1/2 cup), frozen
- Blueberries (3/4 cup), frozen
- Water (1/4 cup)
- Coconut milk (3 tbsp)
- Honey (1 tsp)

Instructions
- In a high-powered blender, combine the banana, strawberries, water, blueberries, coconut milk, protein powder, and honey to make a smooth sorbet.
- Put the sorbet into a cup and top with fresh berries and coconut before ready to consume.

- After pouring the mixture into the serving dish, serve with tacos.

Vegan shortbread cookies
Time: 55 Mins, Serves: 8, Skill: Medium

Ingredients
- Coconut oil (1/4 cup)
- Dried cranberries (1/8 cup), chopped
- Baking soda (1/8 tsp)
- Unbleached flour (1 cup)
- Dried apricots (1/8 cup), chopped
- Powdered sugar (1/2 cup)
- Non-dairy yogurt (2 1/2 tbsp)
- Vanilla extract (1 tsp)
- Pecans (1/8 cup), chopped
- Cardamom (1 tsp), ground
- Pastry wheat flour (1/2 cup)
- Salt (1/4 teaspoon)

Instructions
- Preheat the oven to 325 °F.
- Whisk together yogurt, sugar, and coconut oil, then include cardamom and vanilla to produce a creamy and smooth mixture.
- In a mixing cup, add the flour, salt, and baking soda.
- In a mixing bowl, combine the flour mix and coconut oil mix. To produce a dough, mix the ingredients together with a spoon.
- Combine the nuts and fruits in the dough. Thoroughly knead the dough.
- Make a log out of the dough.
- After covering the logs with parchment paper, place them in the freezer for 30 minutes.
- Cut the logs after they've been frozen and put them in a baking tray lined with parchment paper.
- Bake the cake for 20 minutes, or until baked through.
- Keep in an airtight container after baking.

Crepes with passion fruit
Time: 1 hour and 5 Mins, Serves: 4, Skill: Hard

Ingredients
For crepes:
- Butter (1 1/2 tbsp)
- Unbleached flour (1 cup)
- Oat milk (1 1/4 cups)
- Large eggs (2)

For sauce:
- Sugar (1/2 cup)
- Passion fruit, the pulp (3/4 cup)

Instructions
- In a mixing bowl, whisk together the eggs, milk, and flour. Set the bowl aside.
- In a saucepan, combine the sugar and fruit pulp.
- Over medium heat, bring the fruit pulp mixture to a simmer.
- Reduce the heat to low and continue to cook until the liquid has been reduced to half its original volume. Set it aside for the time being.
- In a crepe tray, melt half a tablespoon of butter over high heat, then pour in crepe batter and spread it out. Cook for about 1 ½ minutes on one side. Cook for another 45 seconds after flipping the crepe.
- When the crepe is finished, transfer it to a serving plate and top it with a spoonful of sauce before folding it in half and serving.

Festive Cranberry Stuffing
Time: 45 Mins, Serves: 2, Skill: Easy

Ingredients
- Apple juice (1/4 cup)
- Stale bread (3 cups)
- Poultry seasoning (1/4 tsp)
- Raw cranberries (1/2 cup)
- Tart apples (1 cup), peeled
- Celery (1/4 cup), chopped
- Unsalted butter (2 tablespoons)

Instructions

- Combine stale bread, sliced apple tart, apple juice, celery, cranberries, poultry seasoning, and butter in a large mixing bowl.
- Bake for 30 minutes at 350 °F in a preheated oven after pouring the batter into a greased casserole dish.

Simple Puerto Rican sofrito

Time: 35 Mins, Serves: 2, Skill: Easy

Ingredients

- Culantro (6 leaves), opt
- Cilantro (1 bunch)
- Garlic cloves (10), chopped
- Green pepper (1), chopped
- Salt (1 tsp)
- Aja peppers (5)
- Spanish Onion (1), chopped

Instructions

- To start, in a blender, puree the onions.
- Combine the green bell pepper, garlic, culantro, dulce pepper, cilantro, and salt in the blender with the onions.
- In an airtight jar, freeze the sofrito.
- Add two teaspoons of sofrito when you are making rice, peas, or soups.

Broccoli blossom

Time: 25 Mins, Serves: 2, Skill: Easy

Ingredients

- Tarragon (1/4 tsp)
- Onion powder (1/4 tsp)
- Ground black pepper, to taste
- Oil (1 tbsp)
- Toasted English muffin (1)
- Onion (1/4 cup), chopped
- Water (3 tbsp)
- Ground red pepper, to taste
- Red cabbage (1 cup), chopped
- Garlic powder (1/4 tsp)

- Broccoli (1/2 cup), chopped
- Parmesan cheese (2 tbsp), grated

Instructions

- In a skillet over medium heat, heat the oil, then add the vegetables and cook for 3 minutes.
- Half-fill the skillet with water and position it over a burner to steam for 5 minutes.
- After 5 minutes, apply the spices and simmer for another 2 minutes.
- Place the vegetables on top of the muffins, serve with parmesan cheese.

Coconut curry cauliflower

Time: 37 Mins, Serves: 4, Skill: Easy

Ingredients

- Olive oil (2 tbsp)
- Lime juice (1/2 lime)
- Cauliflower (1/2 medium)
- Coconut milk (13 1/2 oz.)
- Kosher salt (1/4 tsp)
- Cilantro (1/4 cup), chopped
- Curry paste (1 tsp)

Instructions

- In a pan, heat the oil and add the salt and cauliflower. The cooking time is 7 minutes.
- Pour the coconut milk and curry paste over the cauliflower and cover the pan.
- Set the timer for 10 minutes to boil.
- Season with salt and pepper to taste and garnish with lime juice and cilantro.

Tempeh Pita Sandwiches

Time: 20 Mins, Serves: 4, Skill: Easy

Ingredients

- Tempeh (8 oz.)
- Balsamic vinegar (2 tbsps.)
- Sesame oil (2 tbsps.)
- Onion (1 small)
- Bell pepper, red (1)
- Mayonnaise (4 tsp)

- Pita bread (2 pieces), 6-inch size
- Mushrooms (1/2 cup)

Instructions

- Cut the tempeh into 12 parts. Thinly slice the bell pepper, onion, and mushrooms.
- Heat 1 tablespoon of sesame oil in a large skillet over medium heat. Fry the sliced tempeh for 3 to 4 minutes on either side, until golden brown. After applying the balsamic vinegar, cook for a further minute, then turn them over and cook for another minute. Remove the Tempeh from the skillet.
- Melt the remaining sesame oil over low heat. Add the bell pepper, mushrooms, and onion and cook until they are tender.
- Cut the pita in half to create a pocket. Spread 1 tablespoon of mayonnaise on each half. Place 1/4 of the vegetable blend and 3 slices of tempeh in each half of the pita. Serve immediately.

Citrus Orzo salad

Time: 25 Mins, Serves: 4, Skill: Easy

Ingredients

Dressing

- Parmesan cheese (2 tbsp), grated
- Red pepper flakes (1/4 tsp)
- Lime Juice (2 tbsp)
- Olive oil (1/4 cup)
- Lime zest (1/2 lime)
- Oregano (2 tbsp), chopped

Salad

- Orzo pasta (3 cups), cooked
- Yellow bell pepper (1), diced
- Red bell pepper (1), diced
- Red onion (½), chopped
- Zucchini (1), diced

Instructions

- In a bowl combine the lemon juice, parmesan cheese, olive oil, oregano, lime zest and juice, and flakes, then set it aside.
- In a separate bowl, combine the broccoli, orzo, zucchini, red, and yellow bell peppers.
- Toss the salad with the prepared sauce, mix, and serve.

German braised cabbage

Time: 35 Mins, Serves: 4, Skill: Easy

Ingredients

- Caraway seed (1/2 tsp)
- Apple cider vinegar (3 tbsp)
- Dry mustard (1/2 tsp)
- Olive oil (1 tbsp)
- Chopped pear (1)
- Red cabbage (5 cups), shredded
- Sweet onion (1/4), chopped
- Sugar (1 tbsp)

Instructions

- Cook the onion, cabbage, and pear for 10 minutes in a hot skillet over a high flame.
- Combine the mustard, sugar, vinegar, and caraway seed in a mixing bowl.
- Stir the mustard mixture into the cabbage mixture and thoroughly combine them.
- Simmer for 5 minutes.

Roasted root vegetables

Time: 40 Mins, Serves: 6, Skill: Easy

Ingredients

- Rosemary (1 tsp), chopped
- Turnips (1 cup), chopped
- Parsnips (1 cup), chopped
- Rutabaga (1 cup), chopped
- Extra-virgin olive oil (1 tbsp)
- Black pepper, to taste

Instructions

- Combine the olive oil, rutabaga, turnips, rosemary, and parsnips in a mixing bowl.
- Spread the mixture out on the baking sheet.
- Season with pepper and bake for 25 minutes in a preheated oven at 400 °F.

Greek couscous salad

Time: 30 Mins, Serves: 5, Skill: Easy

Ingredients

- Couscous (3 cups), cooked
- Feta cheese (1/4 cup)
- Cherry tomatoes (1 cup)
- English cucumber (1), diced
- Scallion (1), chopped
- Lemon juice (1 tbsp)
- parsley (2 tbsp), chopped
- Slices of black olives (1/2 cup)
- Balsamic vinegar (2 tbsp)

Instructions

- Combine the tomatoes, olives, mustard, cucumber, lemon juice, scallion, parsley, couscous, vinegar, and feta cheese in a large mixing bowl.

Poultry Recipes

Chicken Veronique

Time: 40 Mins, Serves: 4, Skill: Easy

Ingredients

- Pepper (1/4 tsp)
- Water (1/2 cup)
- Orange marmalade (2 tbsp)
- Bay leaf (1)
- Flour (1 tbsp)
- Halved white grapes (1 cup)
- Pepper (1/4 tsp)
- Unsalted Margarine (6 tbsp)
- White wine (1/4 cup)
- Parsley (1 tsp)
- 1 chicken breast (4oz.)

Instructions

- In a mixing cup, whisk together the flour and 1/4 teaspoon of pepper. Using a thin dusting of flour, gently cover the chicken. In a pan, sauté the chicken in margarine until golden brown.
- Place the remaining components, except for the grapes, in the skillet. Bring to a simmer then add the chicken. Cook for 25 minutes, or until the chicken is cooked through.
- Remove the chicken from the skillet and set aside. Cook the remaining components for a further 2 minutes, stirring continuously, while adding the grapes.
- To serve, drizzle the sauce on top of the chicken.

Barley-Rice Pilaf

Time: 1 Hour and 25 Mins, Serves: 3, Skill: Medium

Ingredients

- Yellow onion (1 small), chopped
- Barley (1/3 cup)
- Pepper (1/8 tsp)
- Margarine (1 tbsp)
- Chicken broth (2 cups), low in sodium
- Carrot (1), peeled & chopped fine
- Stalk celery (1), chopped fine
- White rice (1/3 cup)
- Dried thyme (1/2 tsp)

Instructions

- In a saucepan over low heat, melt the margarine, then add the onion and cook until soft, around 5 minutes.
- Add the rice and barley and bring to a boil for 1 minute.
- Add the remaining ingredients and reduce to a low heat.
- Decrease the heat to low and simmer for 15 minutes, sealed, or until the liquid is gone.

Chicken Salad

Time: 1 Hour and 20 Mins, Serves: 4, Skill: Medium

Ingredients

- Chicken breasts (4), boneless & skinless
- Mayonnaise of Duke (3/4 cup)
- Red grapes (1 cup), seedless and cut in half
- Celery (1/4 cup), chopped
- Red onion (1/4 cup), chopped finely
- Salt (1/4 tsp)
- Black pepper (1/8 tsp)

Instructions

- Combine the chicken with some water in a pot. (Chicken must be covered with water.)
- Cook the chicken for 25 minutes over medium heat, then leave to cool.
- Chop the chicken into small pieces.
- Combine the grapes, chicken, celery, mayonnaise, and onions in a bowl.
- Finish with a pinch of black pepper.

Turkey Salad

Time: 1 Hour and 10 Mins, Serves: 4, Skill: Easy

Ingredients

- Turkey breast (4), boneless & skinless
- Mayonnaise of Duke (3/4 cup)
- Red grapes (1 cup), seedless and cut in half
- Celery (1/4 cup), chopped

- Red onion (1/4 cup), chopped finely
- Salt (1/4 tsp)
- Black pepper (1/8 tsp)

Instructions

- Combine the turkey with some water in a pot. (Turkey must be covered with water.)
- Cook the turkey for 25 minutes in water over medium heat, then leave to cool.
- Chop the turkey into small pieces.
- Combine the grapes, turkey, celery, mayonnaise, and onions in a big mixing bowl.
- Finish with a pinch of black pepper.

Curry Chicken

Time: 1 Hour and 5 Mins, Serves: 4, Skill: Medium

Ingredients

- Dry thyme (1/2 tsp)
- Lemon juice (1/4 cup)
- Onion (1 medium), chopped
- Curry powder (2 tsp)
- Black pepper (1/2 tsp)
- Garlic clove (1 medium), chopped (optional)
- Water (1 cup)
- Chicken (1 whole), cut in small parts, skin removed
- Vegetable or olive oil (2 tbsps.)

Instructions

- After cleaning the chicken, soak it with lemon juice.
- Mix the seasonings in a bowl and rub onto the chicken.
- Marinate the seasoned chicken overnight in the refrigerator.
- Heat the oil in a saucepan and brown the seasoned chicken.
- Add a splash of water to the marinating bowl to preserve marinade.

- Pour the remaining marinade over the browned chicken and cook on low heat until the chicken is tender, about 20 minutes.
- Quickly serve over hot rice.

Easy Chicken and Pasta Dinner

Time: 1 Hour 35 Mins, Serves: 4, Skill: Medium

Ingredients

- Chicken breast (5 oz.), cooked
- Olive oil (1 tbsp)
- Red bell pepper (1/2 cup)
- Zucchini (1 cup)
- Pasta, any shape (2 cups), cooked
- Low-sodium Italian dressing (3 tbsp)

Instructions

- Peel and thinly slice the zucchini and bell pepper.
- In a large skillet, heat the olive oil and cook the peppers and zucchini until soft and crispy, then move to a serving dish.
- Cut the chicken into small strips using a sharp knife.
- Heat the cooked pasta and chicken strips separately in the microwave.
- Toss the pasta with the dressing and eat alongside the sautéed vegetables and chicken strips.

Chicken Waldorf salad

Time: 40 Mins, Serves: 4, Skill: Easy

Ingredients

- Miracle Whip (1/2 cup)
- Chicken (8 oz), cooked & cubed
- Ginger (1/2 tbsp), ground, optional
- Apple (1/2 cup), chopped
- Raisins (2 tbsp)
- Celery (1/2 cup), chopped

Instructions

- Mix all ingredients together carefully.

- It's best to keep it in the fridge for a few hours to allow the flavors to meld.

Salisbury Steak
Time: 1 Hour 30 Mins, Serves: 4, Skill: Medium

Ingredients
- Onion (1 small), chopped
- Black pepper (1 tsp)
- Green pepper (1/2 cup), chopped
- Egg (1)
- Chopped steak, or lean ground beef (1 lb.)
- Vegetable oil (1 tbsp)
- Water (1/2 cup)
- Corn starch (1 tbsp)

Instructions
- Combine the meat, onion, black pepper, egg, and green pepper in a mixing bowl. Once mixed, shape into patties.
- In a pan, heat the oil, then add the patties and sear on all sides.
- After including half of the water, boil for 15 minutes. Remove the patties from the pan and set them aside.
- Combine the beef drippings, remaining water, and corn starch in a pan. Stir the gravy to thicken it as its heating.
- Pour the sauce over the patties and serve right away.

Basic Chicken Loaf
Time: 1 hour and 40 Mins, Serves: 4, Skill: Medium

Ingredients
- Lean chicken (1lb.), ground, boneless
- Green bell pepper (1/2 cup), diced
- Water (1/4 cup)
- Egg white (1)
- Lemon juice (1 tbsp)
- Plain bread crumbs (1/2 cup)
- Onion powder (1/2 tsp)
- Italian seasoning (1/2 tsp)

- Onions (1/2 cup), chopped
- Black pepper (1/4 tsp)

Instructions
- Preheat the oven to 200°F.
- Squeeze the juice of a lemon onto the poultry.
- Mix the remaining components in a dish.
- Gently fold in the meat.
- Cook the loaf in a skillet for 45 minutes.

Stir Fry Meal
Time: 40 Mins, Serves: 4, Skill: Easy

Ingredients
- Frozen stir fry vegetables (1 10-oz. package)
- Low sodium soy sauce (1/2 tbsp)
- Rice (2 cups), cooked
- Cooking oil (2 tbsp)
- Chicken breasts (2 medium), cut in bite-size pieces

Instructions
- Heat the oil in a 9x10' pan on high heat.
- Add the chicken.
- Add the vegetables and toss to combine.
- Mix thoroughly with the soy sauce.
- Lower the heat to medium-high and roast, uncovered, for 3 to 5 minutes, or until the chicken is ready. Stirring occasionally.
- Serve with rice.

Fajitas
Time: 1 hour and 30 Mins, Serves: 6, Skill: Medium

Ingredients
- Dry cilantro (1/2 tsp)
- Flour tortillas (4)
- Vegetable spray
- Vegetable oil (2 tbsp)
- Raw chicken strips (1 1/2 lb.), peeled and deveined
- Chili powder (2 tsp)
- Cumin (1/2 tsp)

- Lemon or lime juice (2 tbsp)
- Green and red pepper (1/4), sliced lengthwise
- White onion (1/2), sliced lengthwise

Instructions

- Preheat the oven to 300°F.
- Heat the vegetable oil in a non-stick pan over medium heat.
- Add the seasonings, lemon or lime juice, and chicken; simmer for 5 to 10 minutes, until meat is tender.
- In a pan, roast the onion and pepper for 1 to 2 minutes.
- Take it off the heat and add the coriander.
- Bake the tortillas covered in foil in the oven. Cook for a maximum of 10 minutes.
- Spoon the tortilla mix into each tortilla, fold as desired and serve.

Giblet Gravy

Time: 40 Mins, Serves: 4, Skill: Easy

Ingredients

- All-purpose flour (1 tbsp)
- Chicken broth (2 cups)
- Poultry liver or giblets (1-2 boiled), chopped
- Hard-boiled egg (1), sliced or chopped

Instructions

- Combine 1 tablespoon of flour with the broth and steam until fluffy.
- In a saucepan, boil the remaining broth over low heat, stirring continuously.
- In a dish, combine the giblets and the egg.
- Stir continuously until the desired thickness is achieved (approximately 5 minutes).

Crunchy Chicken Nuggets

Time: 1 hour and 25 Mins, Serves: 4, Skill: Medium

Ingredients

- Seasoning salt (1/4 tbsp)
- Egg whites (2)
- Melted margarine or butter (1 tbsp)

- Ranch dressing (1 tbsp), reduced-fat, for dipping
- Water (1 tbsp)
- Ready-to-eat crispy rice cereal (2 1/2 cups)
- Paprika (1 1/2 tbsp)
- Chicken breasts (1lb.), boneless, skinless
- Garlic powder (1/8) tbsps.)
- Onion powder (1/8 tbsp)

Instructions

- Mix the egg whites and water in a dish.
- Combine the paprika, crispy rice cereal, powdered onion, salt, and powdered garlic on a large sheet of wax paper.
- Split the chicken into 1 1/2-inch pieces.
- Brush the white egg mixture on all sides of the chicken. Roll the chicken in the cereal blend.
- Place a baking sheet on top of an ungreased baking tin in a single layer. Brush the sheet with a smear of melted butter, then in a single layer add the chicken on top.
- Preheat oven to 450°F and bake for 12 minutes, or until no longer pink in the center.
- Serve immediately with a dipping sauce (reduced-fat ranch dressing).

Low sodium Lemon chicken

Time: 1 hour and 40 Mins, Serves: 4, Skill: Hard

Ingredients

- Chicken breasts (4), boneless, skinless, 1/2-inch thickness
- Fresh ground black pepper (1/2 tsp)
- Lemon juice (2 tbsp)
- Vegetable oil (1 tbsp)
- Lemon (1), sliced
- White wine (1/3 cup)
- Dried oregano (2 tbsp)

Instructions

- Preheat a frying pan for around 2 minutes on medium/high heat. In a mixing cup, combine the oil, white wine, and lemon juice.
- In a pan, toss the chicken breasts in with half of the oregano and half of the pepper, and steam for 3-4 minutes. After flipping the breasts and inserting the remaining oregano and pepper, cook for 3-4 minutes more. According to an instant-read thermometer, the internal temperature must be 165 °F. Remove the chicken from the pan and set it aside.
- Add the lemon slices to the liquid in the skillet and heat for a few minutes, or before the lemons start to caramelize. Reduce the heat to low heat and continue to cook until the mixture has cooled to around half its original temperature.
- Place the chicken on a plate and serve it with the sauce and lemons.

Batty Bites
Time: 1 hour and 20 Mins, Serves: 6, Skill: Medium

Ingredients
- Wheat bread slices (12)
- Smoked turkey (1/2 lb.), sliced
- Catalina dressing

Instructions
- Using a bat-shaped cookie cutter, carve two bat-shaped bats out of a slice of bread.
- Stack two turkey bits together to create bat-shaped cutouts.
- Repeat for the remaining turkey.
- Split the turkey into half of the bread forms (double-stacked).

- Drizzle 1 tablespoon dressing over the turkey and cover with the remaining bread cutouts.

Easy Turkey Sloppy Joes
Time: 1 hour 10 Mins, Serves: 6, Skill: Easy

Ingredients
- Red onion (1/2 cup)
- Hamburger buns (6)
- Brown sugar (2 tbsp).
- Bell pepper green (1/2 cup)
- Turkey, 7% fat, (1-1/2 lb.), ground
- Chicken grilling seasoning blend (1 tbsp)
- Worcestershire sauce (1 tbsp)
- Tomato sauce (1 cup), low-sodium

Instructions
- Chop the bell pepper and onion into tiny bits.
- Combine the vegetables and ground turkey in a wide skillet and cook over medium-high heat until the turkey is completely cooked. Ensure that the solution does not evaporate.
- In a shallow dish, combine the grilling spices, tomato sauce, brown sugar, and Worcestershire sauce.
- Combine the meat and sauce in a large mixing bowl. Reduce the heat to low and cook for another ten minutes.
- Fill burger buns with 6 parts of turkey mixture and serve.

Seafood and Fish Recipes

Baked Salmon

Time: 1 hour and 5 Mins, Serves: 4, Skill: Easy

Ingredients

- Canned pimento (1/4 cup)
- Mayonnaise (1/2 cup)
- Salmon (14 oz.), no salt, drained
- Onion (2/3 cup), chopped
- Plain bread crumbs (1/4 cup)
- Green pepper (1/4 cup), diced
- Grated parmesan cheese (2 tsp)
- Non-stick cooking spray

Instructions

- Preheat the oven to 347 °F.
- Spray a baking tray with nonstick cooking spray.
- Combine the onion, mayonnaise, salmon, pimento, and pepper in a mixing bowl.
- Fill a baking jar halfway with the salmon mixture. On top, sprinkle bread crumbs and Parmesan cheese.
- Bake for 20 minutes, or until the topping is light brown (or until completely heated).

Grilled Trout

Time: 1 hour and 20 Mins, Serves: 2, Skill: Medium

Ingredients

- Lemon pepper (1 tsp), salt free
- Paprika (1/2 tsp)
- Rainbow trout fillets (2 lb.)
- Salt (1/2 tsp)
- Cooking oil (1 tbsp)

Instructions

- Preheat the grill to medium-high.
- Generously oil all sides of the trout fillets. Combine the spices in a bowl. Both fillets should be vigorously rubbed in the spices.
- Place the seasoned trout fillets on the preheated grill, skin side down. Grill for 4 minutes.
- Cook, flipping the fillets halfway through, for 3 to 5 minutes, or until the fish flakes easily with a fork.

Coconut Fish Dream

Time: 40 Mins, Serves: 4, Skill: Easy

Ingredients

- Turmeric (1/2 tbsp), ground
- Cod fillet (450g), cut into large chunks without skin
- Onion (1), chopped and grated
- Coconut milk (300 ml or 1/2-pint), reduced fat
- Garam masala (1/4 tsp)
- Cumin seeds (1 tbsp)
- Margarine/butter (3 tsp), low salt
- Vegetable oil (1 tbsp)
- Green chilies (3), chopped
- Red chili powder (1/2 tbsp)
- Coriander (2 handfuls), chopped

Instructions

- Heat the oil and margarine/butter in a saucepan over low heat.
- Add the onion and cumin seeds, and cook until the onion is tender. Add the green chilies, chili powder, and ground turmeric. Mix together thoroughly.
- Once the sauce is vivid and the oil has spread, add a pinch of garam masala and whisk in the coconut milk. Add the cod and cook for a further 12-15 minutes.
- Garnish with a sprinkling of coriander before eating.
- Serve with rice and a spoonful of green salad.

Broiled Garlic Shrimp

Time: 1 hour, Serves: 4, Skill: Medium

Ingredients

- Pepper (1/8 teaspoon)
- Margarine (1/2 cup), unsalted, melted
- Lemon juice (2 tsp)
- Shrimp in shells (1 lb.)
- Fresh parsley (1 tbsp), chopped
- Onion (2 tbsp), chopped

- Garlic clove (1), minced

Instructions

- Preheat the broiler in the oven. Wash, dry, and peel the shrimp. Combine the margarine, lemon juice, onion, garlic, and pepper in a baking dish.
- Add the shrimp and cover with a lid.
- Cook for 5 minutes under the broiler. Broil for another 5 minutes on the other side.
- Serve on a tray with the pan juices diluted. Serve with a parsley garnish.

Shrimp Fajitas
Time: 45 Mins, Serves: 2, Skill: Easy

Ingredients

- Vegetable oil (2 tbsp)
- Dry cilantro (1/2 tsp)
- Flour tortillas (4)
- Vegetable spray
- Raw shrimp (1 1/2 lb.), peeled and deveined
- Chili powder (2 tsp)
- Cumin (1/2 tsp)
- Lemon or lime juice (2 tbsp)
- Green and red pepper (1/4), sliced lengthwise
- White onion (1/2), sliced lengthwise

Instructions

- Preheat the oven to 300°F.
- In a nonstick tray, heat the vegetable oil over low heat.
- Add the seasonings, lemon or lime juice, and shrimps. Cook for 5 to 10 minutes, or until tender.
- Add the onion and pepper and roast for 1 to 2 minutes.
- Remove the pan from the heat and stir in the coriander.
- Bake the tortillas after arranging them on the foil. Cook for a maximum of 10 minutes.
- Divide the mixture among the tortillas, wrap them and serve.

Spanish Paella
Time: 1 hour 15 Mins, Serves: 2, Skill: Medium

Ingredients

- Red bell pepper (1/3 cup), chopped
- Green onion (1/3 cup), sliced
- Garlic cloves 2, minced
- Pepper (1/4 tsp)
- Chicken breast (1/2 lb.), boneless and skinless, cut into 1/2-inch piece
- Water (1/4 cup)
- Chicken broth (10-1/2-oz can), low in salt
- Medium-size shrimp (1/2 lb.), peeled & cleaned
- Frozen green peas (1/2 cup)
- Ground saffron (a dash)
- White rice, instant (1 cup), uncooked

Instructions

- In a two-quart casserole dish, combine the first three ingredients and cover with the lid. Microwave for 4 to 5 minutes on heavy.
- Combine the shrimp and the remaining ingredients in the casserole dish. Cover and cook for 3 and 1/2 to 4 1/2 minutes on warm, or until the shrimp turns pink.
- Add the rice and mix thoroughly. Cook for 5 minutes, or until the rice is tender.

Shrimp Salad
Time: 1 hour and 20 Mins, Serves: 3, Skill: Hard

Ingredients

- Green pepper (1 tbsp), chopped
- Onion (1 tbsp), chopped
- Tabasco or hot sauce (1/8 tbsp)
- Mayonnaise (2 tbsp)
- Chili powder (1/2 tbsp)
- Lemon juice (1 tbsp)
- Shrimp (1 lb.), chopped, boiled, & deveined
- Hard-boiled egg (1), chopped
- Lettuce, shredded or chopped (optional)
- Celery (1 tbsp), chopped

- Mustard dry (1/2 tbsp)

Instructions

- In a mixing bowl, combine all ingredients except the lettuce and thoroughly blend.
- Chill in the refrigerator for 30 minutes before serving.
- Serve in a lettuce-covered dish or on a sandwich.

Seafood Croquettes
Time: 1 hour and 30 Mins, Serves: 4, Skill: Hard

Ingredients

- Water-packed salmon or tuna (1 can 14.75-oz.)
- Cracker crumbs or plain bread crumb (1/2 cup), unsalted
- Cooking spray or vegetable oil (1) tbsp
- Crab meat (1 lb.), frozen or fresh
- Regular mayonnaise (1/4 cup)
- Egg whites (2)
- Ground mustard (1/2 tbsp)
- Onion (1/4 cup), chopped
- Lemon juice (2 tbsp), optional
- Black pepper (1/2 tbsp)

Instructions

- Drain the canned salmon or tuna.
- In a medium bowl, mix all the ingredients except the oil. Ensuring you mix it rigorously.
- Split the mixture into eight balls and flatten each one to produce patties.
- Heat the vegetable oil in a skillet.
- Slowly lower the patties into the boiling oil.
- Softly brown the patties on both sides. If the patties are fried in grease, drain them on paper towels when cooked.

Salmon Salad
Time: 30 Mins, Serves: 2, Skill: Easy

Ingredients

- Ken's Honey Mustard Dipping Sauce (2 tbsp)
- Celery (1/4 cup), chopped
- Red onion (1/4 cup), chopped

- Red pepper (1/4 cup), chopped
- Canned salmon (12 oz.), low sodium

Instructions

- Chop the celery, red pepper & red onion into small bits.
- Mix it with honey mustard and salmon and serve.

Crab Cakes
Time: 30 Mins, Serves: 4, Skill: Easy

Ingredients

- Garlic powder (1 tsp)
- Egg (1), egg substitute or egg white optional
- Green or red pepper (1/3 cup), finely chopped
- Crackers (1/3 cup), low sodium
- Mayonnaise (1/4 cup), reduced-fat
- Dry mustard (1 tbsp)
- Crushed red pepper or black pepper (1 tsp)
- Lemon juice (2 tbsp)
- Vegetable oil (2 tbsp)

Instructions

- In a mixing bowl, combine all the ingredients.
- Shape patties by dividing the mixture into 6 spheres.
- Heat the vegetable oil in a medium-hot pan or a 347 °F oven.
- In a hot pan, cook the patties for 4 to 5 minutes.
- Serve immediately.

Adobo Marinated Tilapia Tapas
Time: 1 hour, Serves: 4, Skill: Hard

Ingredients

- Nonstick cooking spray
- Wonton wrappers (48), small
- Tilapia filets (6 x 3-oz.)

Adobo Sauce:

- Oregano (1 tbsp)
- Spanish paprika (3 tbsp)
- Olive oil (1/4 cup), extra-virgin
- Black pepper (1 tsp)

- Fresh cilantro (3 tbsp), chopped
- Red wine vinegar (1/2 cup)
- Red pepper flakes (1 tsp)

Slaw Mix:
- Fresh garlic (1 tbsp), chopped
- Mayonnaise (1/2 cup)
- Slaw mix cabbage (4 cups), fresh, shredded
- Lemon juice (1/4 cup)
- Cilantro leaves (1/4 cup), fresh, rough cut
- Green scallions (1/4 cup), fresh, sliced thin on the bias

Instructions
- Preheat the oven to 400 °F.
- In a mixing cup, combine all of the adobo ingredients and set aside.
- Marinate the fish fillets for 30 minutes in half a cup of adobe sauce.
- Coat a baking sheet tray loosely with nonstick cooking spray and bake the fish for 15 minutes at 400°F, turning halfway through. Remove the dish from the oven and put it on a plate to cool.
- In a medium mixing cup, add the mayonnaise, ginger, leftover adobo sauce, cilantro, and scallions. Toss in the cabbage and mix until it is uniformly coated.
- Brush a mini muffin tin with nonstick cooking spray. Using one wonton wrapper to cover the muffin cups.
- Bake the crispy wontons for 5 minutes at 350 °F, then cut them from the tray.
- Divide the fish between the wontons (break or split into 48 pieces) and cover with equivalent quantities of the slaw mixture. Serve with a garnish of cilantro berries.

Creamy Tuna Twist
Time: 25 Mins, Serves: 4, Skill: Easy

Ingredients
- Mayonnaise (3/4 cup)
- Celery pea size (1/2 cup)

- Dill weed (1 tbsp)
- Vinegar (2 tbsp)
- Shell macaroni (1 1/2 cups)
- Tuna (6 1/2 oz.)
- Peas (1/2 cup)

Instructions
- Mix the macaroni shells, mayonnaise, and vinegar thoroughly in a mixing bowl.
- Combine the remaining ingredients in a mixing bowl and stir until well combined.
- Refrigerate for a few hours, covered.

Shrimp-Stuffed Deviled Eggs
Time: 50 Mins, Serves: 6, Skill: Medium

Ingredients
- Eggs (6 large), boiled
- Black pepper (1/4 tsp)
- Shrimp (1/2 cup)
- Mustard (1/2 tsp)
- Mayonnaise (1-1/2 tbsp)
- Lemon juice (1/2 tsp)

Instructions
- Cut the boiled eggs in half lengthwise with a knife. Remove the yolks and place them in a cup with care.
- Finely cut the shrimp and blend in a mixing bowl with the egg yolks, mayonnaise, mustard, lemon juice, and seasoning. Mix thoroughly.
- Position the shrimp and yolk mixture in the egg white halves and serve.

Creamy Shrimp and Broccoli Fettuccine
Time: 1 hour 10 Mins, Serves: 3, Skill: Hard

Ingredients
- Fettuccine (4 oz.)
- Broccoli florets (1-3/4 cup)
- Shrimp (3/4 lb.)
- Garlic clove (1)
- Cream cheese (10 oz.)
- Garlic powder (1/2 tsp)

- Lemon juice (1/4 cup)
- Peppercorns (3/4 tsp)
- Creamer (1/4 cup)
- Red bell pepper (1/4 cup)

Instructions

- Boil the pasta, omitting the salt.
- Add the broccoli after 3 mins of boiling. Drain all excess moisture.
- In a large nonstick pan, cook the shrimp until thoroughly cooked. Add garlic for 2 to 3 mins on medium heat.
- Add the cream cheese, half-and-half, garlic powder, lemon juice, and peppercorns. 2 mins of preparation. Mix thoroughly.
- Toss the shrimp and pasta together. If desired, add the bell pepper.

Fish Sticks

Time: 55 Mins, Serves: 4, Skill: Easy

Ingredients

- Cooking spray
- Tilapia fillets (3 x 1 lb.), cut into 1/2 by 3" strips
- Whole wheat, panko dry breadcrumbs (1 cup), or plain
- Plain cereal flakes, or whole grain (1 cup)
- Lemon pepper (1 tbsp)
- Salt (1/4 tbsp)
- Garlic powder (1/2 tbsp)
- Paprika (1/2 tbsp)
- All-purpose flour (1/2 cup)
- Egg whites (2 large), beaten

Instructions

- Preheat the oven to 450 °F.
- Spray a baking sheet with cooking spray and put it on a wire rack.
- In a food processor, add breadcrumbs, lemon pepper, cereal flakes, paprika, garlic powder, and salt.
- Blend or refine the paste until it is finely ground. Enable to cool in a shallow dish.
- In a second shallow dish, pound the egg whites, and in a third shallow dish, sift the flour.
- Dredge each fish strip in flour, then dip it in the egg and coat all sides in the breadcrumb mix.
- Place the rack that has been prepared into place. Before cooking, spray both sides of the breaded fish with cooking spray.
- Bake for 10 minutes, or until crisp and golden brown.

Salad Recipes

Buttermilk Herb Ranch Dressing
Time: 40 Mins, Serves: 2, Skill: Easy

Ingredients
- Milk (1/2 cup)
- Vinegar (2 tbsp)
- Fresh chives (1 tbsp), chopped
- Dill (1 tbsp)
- Mayonnaise (1/2 cup)
- Oregano Leaves (1 tbsp), chopped
- Garlic powder (1/4 tsp)

Instructions
- Combine the mayonnaise, milk, and vinegar in a medium mixing cup.
- Add 1/4 teaspoon of garlic powder, fresh chives, oregano leaves, and dill.
- Come them together.
- Refrigerate for at least 1 hour to allow flavors to develop.
- To serve, drizzle the dressing on top of a salad.

Crunchy Quinoa Salad
Time: 45 Mins, Serves: 8, Skill: Easy

Ingredients
- Water (2 cups)
- Cucumbers (1/2 cup), seeded and diced
- Quinoa (1 cup), rinsed
- Green onions (3), chopped
- Fresh mint (1/4 cup), chopped
- Lemon rind (1 tbsp), zest
- Olive oil (4 tbsp)
- Parmesan cheese (1/4 cup), grated
- Head Boston or Bibb lettuce (1/2)
- Leaf parsley (1/2 cup), chopped
- Lemon juice (2 tbsp)

Instructions
- Rinse the quinoa under cold running water until it is clean.
- Toast the quinoa for 2 minutes in a skillet over medium-high heat, stirring periodically. Stir in 2 cups of water and bring to a boil, then reduced to low heat, covered, and simmer for 8-10 minutes. Allow a couple of minutes of cooking before fluffing with a fork.
- Combine the mint, parsley, zest, lemon juice, and olive oil with cucumbers, and onions. Toss the quinoa into the blend (cooled).
- Cover lettuce cups halfway with the mixture and top with parmesan cheese.

Violet, Green Salad
Time: 35 Mins, Serves: 4, Skill: Easy

Ingredients
- Sugar snap peas or frozen peas (1 cup)
- Pear (1)
- Goat cheese (3 oz)
- Chive flowers, violets, or edible flowers (1 oz)
- Plain or Greek plain yogurt (1/4 cup)
- Pomegranate molasses (1/4 cup)
- Spring greens (4 cups)
- Cucumber (1)
- Lemon juice (2 tbsp)
- Fresh parsley (1/4 cup)
- Nuts (1/4 cup), optional
- Olive oil (1/2 cup)
- Mustard (1 tsp)
- Allspice (1 pinch)

Instructions
- Cut the greens into bite-sized sections.
- Cucumbers can be split into discs, then quarted.
- To use frozen peas, split the pods in thirds and thaw at room temperature for around half an hour.
- In a mixing dish, combine the diced pear and greens.

- If you have some remaining goat cheese, blend it with the chives and break it into 1/2-inch pieces.
- Combine the yogurt, lemon juice, molasses, parsley, allspice, olive oil, and mustard in a food processor or mixer.
- In a big mixing dish, combine the salad and the dressing.
- For a dazzling show, scatter goat cheese, spices, and nuts around the surface.

Green Beans Salad
Time: 30 Mins, Serves: 4, Skill: Easy

Ingredients
- Oil (1 tbsp)
- Lemon juice (1/2)
- Black pepper, freshly ground, to taste
- Water (12 cups)
- Green beans (1 1/2 lb.), rinsed and ends trimmed

Sauce:

- Honey (1 tbsp)
- Water (1 tbsp)
- Garlic clove (1 large), minced
- Oil (1 tsp)

Instructions
- Get the stockpot's water to a low boil and add the beans. Cook for 3 minutes, or until the beans are light green in color. Be cautious not to overcook them.
- Remove and rinse the beans for 1 minute in cold water. Place the dried beans in a big mixing bowl after they have cooled.
- To create a sauce, blend the honey, garlic, water, and 1 teaspoon of oil in a mixing cup.
- Heat 1 tablespoon of oil in a wide skillet over low heat. Swirl the beans in the oil. Continue to stir for about 3 minutes after adding the sauce.

Green beans that are finished will be bright green and crisp-tender.
- Switch to a serving bowl.
- Now add some pepper (black) and lime juice to enhance the taste.
- Serve and enjoy.

Cabbage with Strawberries
Time: 30 Mins, Serves: 6, Skill: Easy

Ingredients
- Olive or vegetable oil (2 tbsp)
- Cider vinegar (1/4 cup)
- Brown sugar (2 tbsp)
- Fresh Strawberries (1 cup)
- Green Cabbage (1 small)
- Onion (1), coarsely chopped

Instructions
- Sauté the onion in the oil in a wide skillet until softened (nearly 5 minutes).
- Add the vinegar, cinnamon, and sugar; combine the strawberries and cabbage.
- Bring to a boil, then reduce to low heat, cover, and simmer until the cabbage wilts, around 15 minutes.

Creamy Fruit Salad
Time: 25 Mins, Serves: 4, Skill: Easy

Ingredients
- Peaches (2 medium), diced
- Plain Greek yogurt (1 cup)
- Brown sugar cinnamon (2 tsp), to taste
- Lemon (1), juiced
- Strawberries (1 cup), cut in quarters, lengthwise
- Blueberries (1 cup)

Instructions
- In a medium mixing cup, combine all the berries.
- In a small cup, combine the yogurt, lemon juice, and brown cinnamon sugar. To create a full mix, add all the ingredients in a blender.

- Toss the fruit and yogurt mixture together. Combine the products, sample, and change the seasoning as required.
- Refrigerated leftovers can be stored for up to 2 days.

Wild Rice Salad
Time: 1 hour 20 Mins, Serves: 8, Skill: Medium

Ingredients
- Olive oil (1 tbsp)
- Walnuts (2/3 cup), chopped
- Celery rib (4 inches), sliced
- Scallions (4), thinly sliced
- Raisins (2/3 cup)
- Red apple (1 medium), semi-tart, cored and diced
- Pomegranate seeds (1/2 cup)
- Wild rice (1 cup)
- Water (2 cups)
- Lemon zest (1/2 tbsp)
- Lemon juice (3 tbsp)
- Black pepper, freshly ground, to taste
- Olive oil (1/3 cup)
- Sea salt (1/2 tsp)

Instructions
- Clean the wild rice in a strainer of cold water.
- In a medium saucepan, mix it with oil, water, and salt if appropriate. Carry to a boil, then drop to low heat to sustain a gentle simmer.
- Cook for 50 minutes, or until the rice is tender and the liquid has evaporated. If necessary, apply more water after the rice kernels have burst to achieve a soft texture.
- In a large mixing cup, combine the walnuts, scallions, raisins, celery, apples, pomegranate seeds, and lemon zest.
- In a container with a tight-fitting cap, mix the lemon juice, olive oil, and pepper and shake vigorously.

- Toss the apple mixture with half of the dressing and toss well.
- Set the rice aside to cool until it's just mildly moist.
- Serve with the leftover dressing and the fruit combination in a cup or on a lettuce bed at room temperature.

Riced Cauliflower Salad
Time: 35 Mins, Serves: 6, Skill: Easy

Ingredients
- Pomegranate seeds (1/2 cup)
- Almonds (1/2 cup), sliced or chopped
- Mint (1/2 cup), chopped
- Chickpeas (1 cup)
- Cranberries (1/2 cup), dried, sweetened
- Cauliflower (4 1/2 cups), riced
- Lemon (1), zested
- Lemons (2), juiced
- Olive oil (1/4 cup)

Instructions
- Cut the core and leaves from the cauliflower florets and grate them on the wide whole side of a box grater.
- In a big salad bowl, position the riced cauliflower.
- Toss in the pomegranate, mint, almonds, cranberries, chickpeas, and lemon zest.
- Toss the salad with lemon juice and olive oil, gently mixing all ingredients.
- Serve with crisp bread or as a side salad for lunch.

Shrimp Salad with Cucumber Mint
Time: 30 Mins, Serves: 6, Skill: Easy

Ingredients
- Fresh mint leaves (1 cup)
- Lemon juice (2 tbsp)
- Olive oil (3 tbsp)
- Cucumber (1/2), seeded, diced

- Lemon zest (1)
- Med shrimp (2 lb.), cleaned
- Pepper, to taste

Instructions

- Blanch the shrimp for 3 minutes in boiling water, then drain and put aside.
- In a blender or food processor, combine the mint and lemon juice and pulse to coarsely chop the mint.
- Drizzle in the olive oil after pureeing the mint until it is finely sliced.
- Combine the shrimp, mint blend, cucumber, zest, and pepper in a bowl and serve.

Fire and Ice Watermelon Salsa
Time: 25 Mins, Serves: 6, Skill: Easy

Ingredients

- Green bell pepper (1 cup), chopped
- Lime juice (2 tbsp)
- Cilantro (1 tbsp), chopped
- Green onion (1 tbsp), chopped
- Jalapeño (2 meds), seeded and minced
- Garlic clove (1), crushed
- Watermelon (3 cups), chopped

Instructions

- In a large mixing bowl, combine all the ingredients and mix thoroughly.
- Chill for at least an hour before serving.
- Serve with chicken or seafood as a sauce or a dip.

Fruity Chicken Salad
Time: 35 Mins, Serves: 8, Skill: Easy

Ingredients

- Apple (1), cubed
- Raisins (3/4 cup)
- Sour cream (1/2 cup)
- Mayonnaise (1/4 cup)
- Rice vinegar (1 tsp), unseasoned
- Sugar (2 tsp)

- Chicken breasts (2 cups), cooked
- Almonds (1 cup), sliced
- Celery stalk (1), chopped
- Green onion (1), chopped
- Seedless grapes (2 cups)
- Chinese five-spice blend (1/2 tsp)

Instructions

- Combine the chicken, celery, green onion, almonds, grapes, apples, and raisins in a big mixing bowl.
- Blend the sour cream, rice vinegar, mayonnaise, sugar, and Chinese 5-Spice in a separate cup.
- In a mixing bowl, combine the chicken and the dressing.

Lemon Curry Chicken Salad
Time: 25 Mins, Serves: 4, Skill: Easy

Ingredients

- Vegetable oil (1/4 cup)
- Celery (1/2 cup), sliced
- Frozen lemonade concentrate (1/4 cup), thawed
- Ground ginger (1/4 tsp)
- Curry powder (1/4 tsp)
- Garlic powder (1/8 tsp)
- Chicken (1 1/2 cups), cooked and diced
- Grapes (1 1/2 cups), halved

Instructions

- Combine the lemonade concentrate, oil, and spices in a big mixing cup.
- Gently toss in the remaining ingredients.
- Serve after 1 hour marinating.

Cranberry Frozen Salad
Time: 25 Mins, Serves: 4, Skill: Easy

Ingredients

- Vanilla extract (1/2 teaspoon)
- Cranberry sauce (16 oz.), 1 can
- Cream cheese (8 oz.), 1 package

- Whipping cream (1/2 pint)

Instructions

- Melt the cream cheese with a blender.
- In this order, add the whipping cream, vanilla, and cranberry sauce.
- Using a pastry container, pipe it into a 9" x 9" baking tray.
- Freeze.
- To serve, cut the frozen salad into squares.

Purple and Gold Thai Coleslaw
Time: 25 Mins, Serves: 3, Skill: Easy

Ingredients

Dressing:

- Light soy sauce (1 1/2 tbsp)
- Brown sugar (3 tbsp)
- Ginger (2 tbsp), peeled and minced
- Garlic (1/2 tbsp), minced
- Peanut butter (5 tbsp)
- Rice vinegar (5 tbsp)
- Canola oil (5 tbsp)

Slaw:

- Red cabbage (7 cups)
- Yellow pepper (2 cups), sliced or chopped
- Green onions (3/4 cup), sliced
- Fresh cilantro (1/2 bunch)

Instructions

- In a mixing bowl, combine all the dressing components.
- Add the slaw ingredients and the dressing in a wide mixing bowl. Combine thoroughly, and serve.

Beet Salad
Time: 1 hour 20 Mins, Serves: 4, Skill: Medium

Ingredients

- Chilled beets (4), roasted, peeled, and diced
- Walnuts or pecans (1/2 cup)
- Leaf lettuce (1)

- Fresh basil (1/4 cup), chopped fine
- Fruit or herb vinegar (1/2 cup)
- Olive oil (2 tbsp)
- Stilton or blue cheese (2-3 oz.)

Instructions

- Preheat the oven to 400 °F.
- Roast beets for 45 minutes, or until tender.
- Dice and peel the beets once they have cooled.
- In a saucepan, add the nuts, water, and sugar. Boil the fluid, stirring constantly until most of the liquid bubbles have vanished.
- Pour the nuts onto aluminum foil or parchment paper. Separate the nuts when they are still light.
- Enable the components to cool before storing it at room temperature.
- Make a bed of lettuce.
- Combine the beets, balsamic vinegar, basil, and olive oil in a mixing cup.
- Sprinkle it on the bed of lettuce, adding the nuts and cheese on top.

Cool Coconut Marshmallow Salad
Time: 35 Mins, Serves: 6, Skill: Easy

Ingredients

- Dried coconut (1 cup), shredded
- Fruit cocktail (15 oz.), drained
- Fruit-flavored marshmallows (8.8 oz.)
- Sour cream (2 cups)

Instructions

- In a mixing bowl, combine all the ingredients.
- Chill the salad for an hour before eating if you like it creamy. Chill the salad overnight if you want it molded.

Apple Rice Salad
Time: 25 Mins, Serves: 4, Skill: Easy

Ingredients

- Olive oil (1 tbsp)
- Honey (2 tsp)

- Brown/ Dijon mustard (2 tsp)
- Orange peel (1 tbsp), finely shredded
- Garlic powder (1/4 tsp)
- Chilled cooked rice of any kind (2 cups)
- Apples (2 medium), chopped
- Balsamic vinegar (2 tbsp)
- Celery (1 cup), thinly sliced
- Shelled sunflower seeds (2 tbsp), unsalted

Instructions

- Combine the honey, olive oil, orange peel, and garlic powder in a mixing cup and set aside.
- Combine the rice, celery, apples, and sunflower seeds in a large mixing bowl. Toss to ensure it is well combined.
- Toss the rice salad mixture with the seasoning until it is well seasoned.
- Serve immediately, or refrigerate for up to 24 hours.

Snacks & Side Recipes

Anytime Energy Bars
Time: 1 hour and 15 Mins, Serves: 8, Skill: Hard

Ingredients
- Rolled oats (1 cup)
- Eggs (3 large)
- Applesauce (1/3 cup)
- Honey (3 tbsp)
- Cinnamon (1/2 tsp), ground
- Peanuts (3 tbsp), unsalted, chopped
- Semi-sweet small chocolate chips (1/4 cup)
- Coconut (1/3 cup), shredded

Instructions
- Preheat the oven to 325 °F and spray a 9x9-inch baking pan with cooking oil.
- Combine the oats, cinnamon, peanuts, chocolate chips, and coconut in a large mixing cup.
- In a small mixing cup, whisk the eggs. Add the honey and applesauce.
- In a large mixing cup, completely blend the egg and oat mixture.
- Place the mixture evenly onto the rim of the greased pan.
- Cooking time is 40 minutes. Allow it to cool completely before cutting it into bars.

Taco Seasoning
Time: 35 Mins, Serves: 5, Skill: Easy

Ingredients
- Onion powder (1 tbsp)
- Oregano (1 tsp), dried
- Garlic powder (1 tsp)
- Red pepper (1 tsp), crushed
- Cinnamon (1/2 tsp)
- Chili powder (1/4 cup)
- Cumin (1 tbsp), ground

Instructions
- In an airtight jar, combine all the ingredients and store until usage.

Easy baked pears
Time: 45 Mins, Serves: 4, Skill: Easy

Ingredients
- Cinnamon (1/2 tsp), ground
- Clear honey (4 tbsp)
- Ginger biscuits (8)
- Ripe pears (4)
- Crème Fraiche (4 level tbsp), reduced-fat

Instructions
- To start, preheat the oven to 374 °F.
- Split each pear in 1/2. Using a teaspoon, scrape out the cores. In the center of each make a dip. Place them, sliced side up, on the baking sheet.
- Drizzle honey over the top and season with cinnamon.
- Roast the pears for 10 to 15 mins, or until tender. Crush some biscuits of ginger and sprinkle them on top, and serve along with a cream fraiche (spoonful).

Sunshine Carrots
Time: 20 Mins, Serves: 4, Skill: Easy

Ingredients
- Carrots (3 cups), sliced
- Parsley (1 tsp), chopped, fresh, for garnish
- Sugar (1 tbsp)
- Lemon juice (1 tbsp)
- Lemon peel (1/4 tsp), grated
- Margarine (2 tbsp)

Instructions
- Cook the carrots until soft in boiling water; rinse well.
- In a mixing cup, combine the butter, sugar, lemon juice, margarine, and lemon peel.

Southern-fried okra
Time: 45 Mins, Serves: 6, Skill: Easy

Ingredients
- Salt (1/8 tsp)
- Sunflower oil (1/3 cup)

- Yellow cornmeal (1/2 cup)
- Cayenne pepper (1/4 tbsp)
- Black pepper (1/4 tbsp)
- Milk (2 tbsp)
- Egg (1)
- Flour (1/2 cup)
- Okra (3 cups), sliced

Instructions

- Combine the black pepper, flour, salt, cayenne pepper, and cornmeal in a mixing dish.
- In a separate dish, mix the milk and egg.
- Drop the okra parts into the egg mixture, then roll them in the flour mixture before putting them aside.
- In a pan, heat sunflower oil and fry coated okra bits for 2 minutes.
- Or, bake the fried bits for 3 minutes at 300°F in a preheated oven.

Champ – Side Dish Irish Potato
Time: 35 Mins, Serves: 2, Skill: Easy

Ingredients

- Potatoes (600 g)
- Black pepper, ground
- Onions (2), chopped
- Milk (1-2 tbsp)

Instructions

- In a big saucepan of water, boil the potatoes until soft.
- Mash the potatoes once you have added the black pepper, milk, and spring onions.

Slovakian Sauerkraut and Egg Noodles
Time: 55 Mins, Serves: 5, Skill: Easy

Ingredients

- Egg noodles (6 oz.)
- Sauerkraut (4 oz.), drained
- Black pepper (1/2 tsp), ground
- Butter (2 tbsp), unsalted
- Onion (1/2 small/35g), diced

- Dill (1 tbsp), fresh, chopped

Instructions

- Melt one tablespoon of butter over medium heat in a large skillet
- Add the onions. Cook, stirring regularly, until the onions are smooth and transparent, around 5 minutes.
- Put a broad pot halfway full of water to a boil.
- Add the egg noodles to the boiling broth and cook as directed on the box.
- Add the sauerkraut and 1/2 tablespoon more butter to the fried onions. Since thoroughly blending, boil for 3 minutes.
- Combine the noodles, sauerkraut, and the remaining 1/2 tablespoon of butter in the same pan. Blend well after seasoning with black pepper.
- Garnish with dill on top. You should serve it with a side salad.

Deviled Eggs
Time: 45 Mins, Serves: 8, Skill: Easy

Ingredients

- Cider vinegar (1 tsp)
- White sugar (1 tsp)
- Yellow mustard (1 tsp)
- Onion powder (1/2 tsp)
- Eggs (6), hard-boiled
- Mayonnaise (2 tbsp)

Instructions

- Halve the eggs and set aside the whites and yolks separately.
- In a shallow bowl, mash the yolks with a fork. Add the mayonnaise, vinegar, onion powder, and mustard. Blend until fully smooth.
- Place the mixture in a piping bag and pipe it into the egg white halves.
- If necessary, garnish with paprika. Refrigerate before serving.

Swiss Chard Crostini
Time: 35 Mins, Serves: 10, Skill: Easy

Ingredients
- Olive oil (2 tbsp)
- Garlic cloves (3)
- Water (3 tbsp)
- Baguette (1/2), sliced into 10, ½-inch slices
- Swiss chard (1/2 bunch/6 oz.)
- Ricotta cheese (1/2 cup)

Instructions
- Toast the baguette slices until finely browned in a toaster oven or a standard oven at 300°F.
- Extract the Swiss chard's roots. To build a leaf mound, arrange the leaves in four layers. Roll horizontally and slice into the rolls to create leaf ribbons.
- Continue until all the leaves are trimmed.
- Melt the olive oil in a large skillet over medium heat. For 2 minutes, stirring halfway through, roast the Swiss chard and garlic. Reduce to a low heat and place in boiling water. Cook until the chard is soft but still has a light green color.
- Position the toasted baguette slices on a serving tray to assemble. Spread a thin layer of ricotta on each piece. Place the cooked chard on top of the ricotta toast with tongs. Serve as a snack or an appetizer.

Spiced Pepitas
Time: 40 Mins, Serves: 8, Skill: Easy

Ingredients
- Brown sugar (1 tbsp)
- Cumin seed (1 tsp), grounded
- Butter (1 1/2 tbsp), unsalted
- Pepitas (1 1/2 cups)

Instructions
- In a skillet over low heat, melt the butter, then stir in the sugar and cumin until well combined.
- To fairly spread the pepitas, apply them and combine for 1 to 2 minutes.
- Remove the pan from the heat and set it aside to cool.
- Any serving may be enjoyed alone, or with a slice of fruit or cheese as a snack.

BBQ Asparagus
Time: 1 hour 10 Mins, Serves: 6, Skill: Easy

Ingredients
- Pepper (1-1 1/2 tsp)
- Lemon juice (2-3 tbsp)
- Asparagus (1-1 1/2 lb.), fresh, 12 to 15 large spears
- Extra-virgin olive oil (2-3 tbsp)

Instructions
- In a shallow dish large enough to roll the asparagus in, combine the oil, pepper, and lemon juice and cover entirely with the mixture.
- Clean and trim the woody ends of the asparagus spears.
- Set aside in the tub after rolling the asparagus in the oil mixture. Place the tray on a platter in the refrigerator to marinate until the grill is primed.
- Prepare the barbecue or gas grill by lighting it and positioning it over a medium-high flame.
- To prevent the spears from sticking to the plate, gently spray the vegetable grilling tray or a grill basket into a shallow dish with olive oil spray.
- Arrange the asparagus spears on a vegetable grilling plate and drizzle the leftover oil from the dish over the other.
- Grill the asparagus in a skillet, or on tin foil until soft and starting to brown, around 5 minutes. At room temperature or a higher temperature, serve.

BBQ Corn on the Cob
Time: 45 Mins, Serves: 8, Skill: Easy

Ingredients
- Thyme (1 tsp), dried
- Parsley (1 tsp)
- Black pepper (1/2 tsp)

- Corn on the cob (4)
- Olive oil (3 tbsp)
- Parmesan cheese, grated

Instructions
- In a big enough dish to roll the corn into and completely coat it with the mixture, combine the oil, cheese, parsley, thyme, and black pepper.
- Roll the corn cob in the mixture to fully coat it.
- All of the mix should be put in the middle of a heavy-duty aluminum foil sheet.
- Fold the foil sheet's sides together to create a pan, ensuring that no oil spills onto the grill.
- Place the foil tray on the grill over medium heat for 15-20 minutes, rotating halfway through to ensure even browning on both sides.

Not Very Spicy Chipotle Wings
Time: 1 hour, Serves: 4, Skill: Easy

Ingredients
- Butter (1/4 cup), unsalted, slightly melted
- Black pepper (1 tsp)
- Chives (1 tbsp), chopped
- Jumbo chicken wings (1 lb.), fresh
- Chipotle peppers (1 1/2 tbsp), diced, in adobo sauce*
- Honey (1/4 cup)

Instructions
- Preheat the oven to 400 °F.
- Arrange the precut wings on a baking tray lined with greased baking sheets.
- Bake for 20 minutes, or until crisp on the outside and an internal temperature of 165 °F, using an instant-read thermometer halfway through.
- In a mixing cup, combine the remaining ingredients and whisk briefly with a rubber spatula before mixing.

- Take the wings out of the oven and toss them in the sauce to cover them equally. Serve immediately on a big platter.

Sweet Spice Cottage Cheese
Time: 25 Mins, Serves: 4, Skill: Easy

Ingredients
- Cottage cheese (4 oz.), no-salt-added, 1%
- Cinnamon (1/2 tsp)
- Honey (2 tsp)
- Apple (1/2 small), chopped

Instructions
- Add the cottage cheese, apple, and cinnamon to a mixing dish. To create a full mix, add all the ingredients to a blender.
- Serve with honey drizzled on top.

Cauliflower in Mustard Sauce
Time: 50 Mins, Serves: 4, Skill: Easy

Ingredients
- White-wine vinegar (3 tbsp)
- Olive oil (1 tbsp)
- Black pepper (a dash)
- Cauliflower (2 cups)
- Dijon mustard (2 tsp)
- Honey (1 tsp)

Instructions
- In a mixing cup, add the mustard, honey, vinegar, and olive oil.
- Apply a tablespoon of black pepper to taste.
- Cook the cauliflower until it is soft in hot water.
- Drain all the water.
- Toss the grilled cauliflower with the dressing after it has been soaked.
- Allow to cool for 30-45 minutes before serving.

Meat Recipes

Beef Casserole

Time: 40 Mins, Serves: 2, Skill: Easy

Ingredients

- Salt (1/4 tsp)
- Fresh parsley (1 tbsp), chopped
- Lean beef (500g)
- Water (350ml)
- Onion (1 medium), chopped
- Vegetable oil (1 tbsp)
- Carrots (2 medium), peeled and sliced
- White pepper (1/4 tsp)

Instructions

- Fry the onion in a limited volume of vegetable oil.
- Add the beef and cook until it is browned.
- Then add some water and cook until the beef is tender.
- Add the carrots and onions to the meat and proceed to cook until the vegetables and the meat are cooked through.
- Apply salt, pepper, and finely chopped parsley to taste.

Beef Curry

Time: 3 hours, Serves: 4, Skill: Hard

Ingredients

- Vegetable oil (5 tbsp)
- Beef with bone (1-1/2 lb.), small
- Whole cumin seeds (3/4 tsp)
- Salt (3/4 tsp)
- Bay leaves (2)
- Whole peppercorns (1/4 tsp)
- Cayenne pepper (1-1/2 tsp)
- Cinnamon stick (1)
- Garam masala (1/2 tsp)
- Tomato (1 medium)
- Garlic cloves (2)
- Onions (2 medium)
- Ginger root (1" cube)

Instructions

- Peel and chop the tomato. Mince the garlic, pepper, and ginger root.
- Heat the oil in a large, thick pot over medium-high heat. Add the cumin seeds, bay leaves, cinnamon sticks, and peppercorns, stirring occasionally.
- Add the garlic, ginger, and onion, and cook until brown specks appear on the onion.
- Add the beef, cabbage, cayenne pepper, flour, and a quarter cup of water to the pan and blend well. Bring to a low simmer, stirring regularly.
- Cover the pan, lower the heat to low, and simmer for 45 minutes, or until the beef is tender and juicy. Continue to stir during the cooking period.
- Remove the cover and maintain a low heat. To minimize the amount of oil used, season with garam masala and fry, stirring periodically, for around 5 minutes.

Hawaiian-Style Slow-Cooked Beef

Time: 6 Hours, Serves: 4, Skill: Hard

Ingredients

- Onion powder (1 tsp)
- Paprika (1/2 tsp)
- Liquid smoke (2 tbsp)
- Boneless Beef (4 lb.)
- Black pepper (1/2 tsp), freshly ground
- Pickled or radishes red onions (optional garnish)
- Garlic powder (1/2 tsp)

Instructions

- In a bag, add black pepper, paprika, garlic powder, and onion.
- Rub the beef with the flavoring paste all over. In a slow cooker or a cooker, position the beef. Sprinkle with liquid smoke.
- Pour sufficient water into the crock-pot or slow cooker to fill it to a depth of 14–12 inches. Cook for 4–5 hours on high pressure.

- Shred the beef with two forks after extracting it from the cooker.
- Serve it warm.

Fiesta Lime Tacos
Time: 14 Mins, Serves: 12, Skill: Easy

Ingredients
- Water (3/4 cup)
- Lean ground beef or turkey (1 lb.)
- Mrs. Dash Fiesta Lime Seasoning Blend (4 tbsp)
- Taco shells (12), or 6-inch flour tortillas

Instructions
- Brown the ground beef in a large skillet over medium-high heat.
- Get rid of the excess fat.
- Add the water and Mrs. Dash Fiesta Lime Seasoning Mixture.
- Bring the water to a boil. Reduce the heat to low and simmer, stirring occasionally, for 5 minutes.
- Scoop the meat mixture into taco shells or tortillas that are already soft. If chosen, serve with additional toppings.

Seasoned Pork Chops
Time: 1 hour and 10 Mins, Serves: 3, Skill: Hard

Ingredients
- Lean pork chops (4 x 4-ounce), fat removed
- Vegetable oil (2 tbsp)
- Thyme (1/2 tbsp)
- All-purpose flour (1/4 cup)
- Black pepper (1 tsp)
- Sage (1/2 tbsp)

Instructions
- Preheat the oven to 350 °F.
- Spray the skillet with cooking spray.
- In a mixing dish, combine the flour, sage, black pepper, and thyme.
- Dredge the chops in the flour mix and drop them in the baking tray with the oil.

- Put it in the oven for about 40 minutes, or until it is juicy on all sides.

Parsley Burger
Time: 1 hour and 10 Mins, Serves: 1, Skill: Medium

Ingredients
- Oregano (1/4 tbsp)
- Slender ground turkey or beef (1 lb.)
- Thyme (1/4 tbsp), ground
- Lemon juice (1 tbsp)
- Black pepper (1/4 tbsp)
- Parsley flakes (1 tbsp)

Instructions
- Gently blend all the ingredients in a large mixing cup.
- Shape into four small patties, each around 3/4 inches in diameter.
- Put in a skillet or broiler pan that has been finely greased.
- Broil for 10 to 15 minutes after turning, about 3" from the flame.

Easy Beef Burgers
Time: 1 hour 10 Mins, Serves: 2, Skill: Medium

Ingredients
- Dried mixed herbs (a pinch)
- Onion (1), chopped
- Black pepper
- Beef or pork (500 g), low in fat, minced

Instruction:
- Ready the grill or barbecue by preheating it. Combine all the ingredients in a big mixing cup.
- Using clean, damp hands, split it into 8 small or 4 large patties. Cut the beef into flattish rounds of similar depth to ensure even and detailed cooking.
- Cook for 5 to 10 minutes on either side on the grill.
- Both the inside and outside of the burgers must be brown. Serve on pita bread or a sandwich

bun with sliced lettuce and a spoonful of mayonnaise, tomato sauce, or vinegar.

Tortilla Beef Rollups
Time: 25 Mins, Serves: 2, Skill: Easy

Ingredients
- Romaine lettuce leaves (2)
- Roast beef (5 oz.), cooked
- Red onion (1/4 cup), chopped
- Cucumber (8 slices)
- Flour tortilla (2), 6" size
- Red/Green or Yellow bell pepper (1/4), cut in strips
- Cream cheese (2 tbsp), whipped
- Herb seasoning blend (1 tbsp)

Instructions
- Place the tortillas on a plate and spread cream cheese on top.
- Split the products in half to produce two tortillas. On each tortilla, layer the roast beef, pepper strips, red onion, cucumbers, & lettuce.
- Season with a pinch of salt and pepper.
- Fold tortillas.
- Serve each tortilla whole or cut into 4 parts.

Jamaican Beef Patties
Time: 1 hour and 20 Mins, Serves: 2, Skill: Medium

Ingredients
- Garlic clove (1), chopped
- Fresh chili (1), minced
- Chili powder (1 tbsp.)
- Thyme (1/2 tbsp), dried
- Short crust pastry (500g or 1 lb.), one packet
- Beef (200g or 8oz.), minced
- Breadcrumbs (4 tbsp), 2 slices of bread
- Onion (1 small), chopped
- Curry powder (1 tbsp)

Instruction:
- Preheat the oven to 400°F.

- Cook the chopped garlic and onion with the minced beef in a nonstick frying pan until the meat is nearly brown. Cook for 15 minutes with the breadcrumbs and seasoning, covered, over a low flame. Using a colander or sieve, drain and remove any remaining liquid.
- On a saucer, roll out the pastry to make 6 circles.
- Divide the beef evenly among the pastry rings. To close the pastry, dampen the sides, cut it in half, and press the corners together. Rub it with milk and place it on a baking tray.
- Bake for 25-30 minutes, or until golden brown, in the center of the oven.

Chili Rice with Beef
Time: 50 Mins, Serves: 1, Skill: Easy

Ingredients
- Rice (2 cups), cooked
- Onion (1 cup), chopped
- Black pepper (1/8 tsp)
- Chili con carne seasoning powder (1 1/2 tsp)
- Sage (1/2 tsp)
- Ground beef (1 lb.), lean
- Vegetable oil (2 tbsp)

Instructions
- In a skillet, heat the oil and add the beef and onion. Fry until golden brown, stirring constantly.
- Apply fried rice and spices to the combination. S
- Remove the combination from the flames. Cover with a lid and set aside for 10-14 minutes.

Lamb Chops and Mustard Sauce
Time: 45 Mins, Serves: 2, Skill: Medium

Ingredients
- Garlic clove (1), minced
- Orange (1 tsp), grated and peeled
- Dry rosemary (1 tsp)
- Water (1 tbsp)

- Lamb chops (2/12 oz.)
- Seasoning of Mrs. Dash herb (1/2 tsp)
- Brown mustard (1 tsp), spicy
- Orange marmalade (2 tbsp), reduced-sugar

Instructions

- In a mixing cup, finely chop the garlic and combine it with seasoning of Mrs. Dash and rosemary.
- Scatter on the top of the lamb chops.
- Broil for 5 minutes on either side, 6 inches apart.
- In a shallow dish combine the mustard, orange peel, water, and marmalade.
- Combine all ingredients in a microwave-safe bowl and heat for 1 minute.
- Brush the sauce over the broiled chops and broil for 1 minute.

Cranberry Pork Roast

Time: 12 Hours and 45 Mins, Serves: 4, Skill: Hard

Ingredients

- Salt (1/2 tsp)
- Pork roast (4 lb.), center-cut
- Orange peel (1 tsp), zest, grated
- Cranberries (1 cup), chopped
- Nutmeg (1/8 tsp)
- Black pepper (1 tsp)
- Honey (1/4 cup)
- Brown sugar (1 tbsp)
- Garlic cloves (1/8 tsp), ground

Instructions

- Sprinkle the pork roast with pepper and salt. Put it in a crock-pot or slow cooker.
- Add the rest of the ingredients and pour over roast.
- Cover and simmer for 8-10 hours on low.
- From the crock-pot or slow cooker, cut the roast and slice it into 24 pieces. Cover it with a spoonful of drippings.

Pork Pasties

Time: 1 hour and 20 Mins, Serves: 4, Skill: Hard

Ingredients

- Potato (1 medium/100g)
- White/ Black pepper
- Carrot (1 medium)
- Pork (200g), minced
- Dried herbs
- Short crust pastry (500g), one packet
- Onion (1 small)

Instruction:

- Preheat oven to 400 °F.
- Brown the pork in a saucepan (non-stick). Cook for 15 minutes, or until the meat is halfway cooked. Eliminate any residual liquid from the meat.
- Boil the potatoes, carrots, and onion for 10 minutes, then drain well and break into small bits. Toss the mince in a big mixing tub. As required, season the meat with pepper and herbs.
- On a saucer, roll out the pastry to produce 6 circles.
- Divide the meat among the pastry rings, dampen the pastry corners, fold in half, and press the pastry corners together to seal. Rub it with milk and place it on a baking tray.
- Bake for 25-30 minutes in the center of the oven.

Onion Smothered Steak

Time: 1 hour and 35 Mins, Serves: 4, Skill: Hard

Ingredients

- Vinegar (1 tbsp)
- Garlic clove (1), minced
- Flour (1/4 cup)
- Bay leaf (1)
- Dried thyme (1/4 tsp), crushed
- Round steak (1 1/2 lb.), 3/4" thick
- Oil (2 tbsp)

- Pepper (1/8 tsp)
- Water (1 cup)
- Onions (3), sliced

Instructions

- Cut the steak into 8 separate halves with a sharp knife. Pound the flour and pepper onto the steak with your fingers.
- Brown the meat in oil in a skillet (both sides). Put it on a plate and set it aside.
- In a skillet, combine the garlic, vinegar, bay leaf, and thyme. Simply get it to low heat.
- Put the meat in the middle of the mixture and top with the sliced onions. With the cover down, cook for an hour.

Chili Con Carne

Time: 1 hour and 45 Mins, Serves: 2, Skill: Hard

Ingredients

- Garlic powder (1 tsp)
- Ground cumin (1/2 tsp)
- Water (1/4 liter.)
- Lean ground beef (1 lb.)
- Onion (1 cup), chopped
- Green pepper (1/2 cup), chopped
- Chili powder (2 tbsp)
- Paprika (1/2 tsp)

Instructions

- Brown the beef in a pot. Drain all unnecessary fat. Add the green pepper and onion.
- Continue to cook until the onion is translucent. After including the remaining ingredients, cook for 1 hour and 30 minutes.
- measure the chili and add enough water to create 5 cups before serving.

Soup & Stew Recipes

Thai Chicken Soup

Time: 50 Mins, Serves: 4, Skill: Easy

Ingredients

- Sugar (1 tbsp), brown/white
- Chili sauce/chili flakes (1 tsp)
- Lemongrass stalk (1), chopped
- Ginger (1"), sliced
- Lite coconut milk (1 can)
- White button mushrooms (10), quartered
- Red bell pepper (1), sliced
- Yellow onion (1/2), sliced
- Lime juice (2 tbsp)
- Chicken breast (1 lb.), or shrimp
- Simple Chicken Broth (4 cups), other low sodium broth
- Fish sauce (1/2 tbsp)

Instructions

- In a large pot coated with nonstick cooking oil, brown the shrimp or chicken until evenly browned.
- Add the broth, fish sauce, chili sauce, ginger, and lemongrass.
- Reduce the heat to medium-low and cook for 10 to 15 minutes, stirring periodically.
- Add the coconut milk, bell pepper, mushrooms, and onions. Simmer for 5 minutes.
- Lime juice can be added just before serving.

Wild Rice Soup

Time: 1 hour and 5 Mins, Serves: 4, Skill: Medium

Ingredients

- Red onion (1 cup), diced small
- Garlic powder (1 1/2 tsp)
- Dried thyme (1/2 tsp)
- Pepper (1/4 tsp)
- Salt (1/2 tsp)
- Wild rice (1/2 cup), dry
- Water (6 cups)
- Olive oil (1 tbsp)
- Celery (1/2 cup), sliced
- Kale (2 cups), stemmed & leaves chopped
- Parsley (1/4 cup), chopped
- Lemon juice (1 tbsp)

Instructions

- In a wide pot, heat the oil, then add the onions and celery and cook, stirring occasionally, for 3 to 4 minutes, or until slightly brown.
- Add the seasonings, garlic powder, salt, dried thyme, and pepper. Cook for about 30 seconds, or until fragrant, stirring constantly.
- Toast the wild rice for at least 2 minutes after mixing it in.
- In the water, mix it together. Bring to a simmer, sealed, over high flame.
- Reduce heat to low and simmer for around 50 minutes, stirring regularly, until it starts to boil.
- Cook for another 5 minutes after adding the kale.
- Add the parsley and lemon juice. Pots may be used to prepare the soup.

Minestrone Soup

Time: 1 hour and 20 Mins, Serves: 4, Skill: Medium

Ingredients

- Onion (1/2 large), diced
- Garlic cloves (4), minced
- Italian seasoning (1 tsp)
- Black pepper (1/2 tsp)
- Vegetable stock (4 cups), no-salt-added
- Tomatoes (14.5 oz.), diced, no-salt-added, 1 can
- Mixed vegetables (10 oz.), frozen
- Olive oil (2 tbsp)
- Short, dried pasta, like ditalini (3 oz.)

Instructions

- Heat the liquid in a broad pot over medium-low heat. Cook the garlic, onion, pepper, and Italian seasoning, stirring occasionally. About 8 minutes.
- Allow the onions, mixed vegetables, and tomatoes to boil in the cooker. Cook until the dry pasta is just under al dente.
- Serve immediately.

Quick Mushroom Broth

Time: 40 Mins, Serves: 2, Skill: Easy

Ingredients

- Dried mushrooms (5-8)
- Water (2-4 cups)
- Onions (1/2 cup), chopped
- Carrots & celery (1/2 cup), chopped

Instructions

- In a saucepan, bring all ingredients to a boil, then reduce heat to low and enable to simmer for 10 minutes.

Chicken and Corn Chowder

Time: 40 Mins, Serves: 12, Skill: Easy

Ingredients

- Chicken breasts (8), boneless, diced
- Fresh thyme (6 tbsp), chopped
- Bacon (12 slices), low sodium
- Onions (2), chopped
- Chicken broth (7 cups), low sodium
- Potatoes (4), diced & soaked
- Corn (8 cups)
- Mocha Mix (4 cups)
- Black pepper (1/2 tsp)
- Green onions (8), chopped

Instructions

- Fry the bacon. Remove the bacon from the pan and place it on a plate to cool.
- Fry the onions in the bacon fat.
- After including the potatoes and broth, cover and simmer for 10 minutes.
- Add the chicken, corn, and thyme to the pot and cook until the chicken is thoroughly baked, (15 mins).
- Add the Mocha Mix to the broth, cook for 2 minutes.
- Toss in the bacon, green onions, and season to taste with salt and pepper.

Simple Soup Base

Time: 1 hour, Serves: 4, Skill: Easy

Ingredients

- Paprika (1/4 tsp)
- Flour (2 tbsp)
- Margarine or butter (2 tbsp)
- Milk (2 cups)
- Dry mustard (1/4 tsp)
- Parsley, basil or any other herbs (1/2 tsp)

Instructions

- Mix margarine and flour in a microwave-safe dish.
- Microwave for 30 seconds on high, stir, then microwave for another 30 seconds on high.
- Add the spices and milk, and cook for another minute in the microwave.
- To thicken, microwave for another minute. Microwave for a further minute if the sauce isn't thick enough.
- It may be used in lieu of cream soups.

Texas-Style Chili

Time: 1 hour and 25 Mins, Serves: 6, Skill: Hard

Ingredients

- Onion (1 large)
- Tomato sauce (8 oz.), 1 can, unsalted if possible
- Water (2 cups)
- Green chili pepper (4 oz.), 1 can
- Red bell pepper (1), chopped
- Chili powder (2 tbsp)

- Lean ground beef (1 lb.)
- Garlic powder (1 tbsp)
- Cumin (1/4 tsp), ground
- Dried oregano (1/2 tsp)
- Dried thyme (1/2 tsp)
- Dried basil (1 tsp)
- Cajun seasoning (1/4 tsp)

Instructions

- In a big pot over medium heat, brown the beef.
- Add the onion and cook until it is soft, around 5 minutes.
- In a big mixing bowl, add 2 cups water, tomato sauce, bell pepper, green chilies, and spices.
- Bring to a simmer, then reduce to low heat and proceed to cook for around 1 hour.

Vibrant carrot soup

Time: 1 hour, Serves: 4, Skill: Easy

Ingredients

- Olive oil (1 tbsp)
- Ginger (2 tsp), grated
- Sweet onion (1/2), chopped
- Garlic (1 tsp), minced
- Carrots (3), chopped
- Water (4 cups)
- Coconut milk (1/2 cup)
- Turmeric (1 tsp), ground
- Cilantro (1 tbsp), chopped

Instructions

- Sauté the garlic, onion, and ginger in a saucepan of hot olive oil for 3 minutes over a high flame.
- Bring the turmeric, water, and carrots to a boil in a saucepan.
- Reduce the heat to low and proceed to cook for another 20 minutes.
- Put the soup mixture and vegetables into a blender and add the coconut milk to produce a smooth broth.

- Return the smooth soup mixture to the pan and heat until it has thickened to the consistency of a deep soup.
- Garnish with chopped cilantro.

Green Breakfast Soup

Time: 40 Mins, Serves: 2, Skill: Easy

Ingredients

- Vegetable broth (2 cups)
- Coriander (1 tsp), ground
- Turmeric (1 tsp), Ground
- Cumin (1 tsp), ground
- Lettuce (1 cup)
- Black pepper, to taste

Instructions

- Mix the lettuce, coriander, turmeric, broth, and cumin in a food processor.
- Transfer the mixture to a skillet and cook over medium heat for 3 minutes.
- Season to taste with pepper and serve.

Vegetable Stew

Time: 50 Mins, Serves: 8, Skill: Easy

Ingredients

- Cayenne pepper (1 pinch)
- Garlic (1 tsp), chopped
- Red bell pepper (1), diced
- Tomatoes (2), chopped
- Coriander (1 tsp)
- Carrots (2), chopped
- Cumin (1/2 tsp)
- Zucchini (2), chopped
- Broccoli florets (2 cups)
- Onion (1), chopped
- Black pepper, to taste
- Olive oil (1 tsp)
- Cilantro (2 tbsp), chopped
- Vegetable stock (2 cups)

Instructions

- Heat the olive oil in a medium saucepan and sauté the garlic and onion.
- After adding the bell pepper, zucchini, and carrots, cook for another 5 minutes.
- Add the tomatoes, cumin, broccoli, cayenne pepper, and coriander.
- Reduce it to a low heat.
- Proceed to cook the vegetables for another 5 minutes.
- Garnish with cilantro and black pepper before serving.

Mediterranean Soup Jar

Time: 40 Mins, Serves: 2, Skill: Easy

Ingredients

- Bell pepper and onion strips (1/2 cup), fresh or frozen
- Black olives (3 large), reduced sodium
- Ricotta cheese (1 tbsp), whole milk
- Canned chickpeas (1/3 cup), no salt added
- Garlic and herb seasoning blend (1/2 tbsp)
- Black pepper (1/2 tsp)
- Red pepper flakes (1/8 tbsp)
- Extra-virgin olive oil (1 tbsp)
- Coleslaw mix (1/2 cup)

Instructions

- Rinse the chickpeas and cut the black olives in half.
- In a 16-ounce glass jar, layer all the ingredients in the order mentioned above.
- Refrigerate it before you're able to cook and serve it.
- Remove the container from the refrigerator 15 minutes before serving.
- Fill the container halfway with boiling water, shut the lid, and shake to mix. Allow 2 minutes for the ingredients to settle in the jar.
- Fill a large bowl halfway with the contents and serve.

Rotisserie Chicken Noodle Soup

Time: 45 Mins, Serves: 4, Skill: Easy

Ingredients

- Carrots (1 cup)
- Wide noodles (6 oz.), uncooked
- Onion (1/2 cup)
- Rotisserie chicken (1), prepared
- Chicken broth (8 cups), low-sodium
- Celery (1 cup)
- Fresh parsley (3 tbsps.)

Instructions

- After deboning the chicken, cut it into bite-sized pieces. Prepare 4 cups of broth for the soup.
- Fill a stockpot halfway with chicken broth and bring to a boil.
- Cut the celery and carrots into thin slices and dice the onion.
- Add the chicken, vegetables, and noodles.
- Bring to a boil, then reduce to low heat and cook for around 15 minutes, or until the noodles are finished.
- Serve with sliced parsley as a garnish.

Chicken Pot Pie Stew

Time: 1 hour 10 Mins, Serves: 6, Skill: Medium

Ingredients

- Canola oil (1/4 cup)
- Chicken breast (1 1/2 lb.), boneless, skinless
- Heavy cream (1/2 cup)
- Sweet peas (1/2 cup), frozen, thawed
- Piecrust (1), frozen, cooked, and broken into bite-size pieces
- Chicken stock (2 cups), low-sodium
- Fresh onions (1/2 cup), diced
- Flour (1/2 cup)
- Fresh carrots (1/2 cup), diced
- Black pepper (1/2 tsp)
- Chicken bouillon (2 tsp), low sodium
- Cheddar cheese (1 cup), low-fat

- Fresh celery (1/4 cup), diced
- Italian seasoning (1 tbsp), sodium-free

Instructions

- Pound the chicken and cut it into tiny cubes to tenderize it.
- Cook for half an hour over medium-high heat with the chicken and stock in a large stockpot. In the meantime, blitz the flour and oil together in a blender until smooth.
- Slowly stir in the flour and pour it into the chicken broth mixture until it slightly thickens. For 15 minutes, reduce the heat to medium-low or low.
- Add the bouillon, onions, celery, carrots, Italian seasoning, and black pepper. Cook for 15 minutes more.
- Take the pan from the heat and whisk in the milk and peas. Mix until it's absolutely smooth. Serve in mugs filled with equal parts cheese and piecrust.

Potato Soup, Irish Baked

Time: 40 Mins, Serves: 6, Skill: Easy

Ingredients

- Potatoes (2 large)
- Cheese (4 oz.), cubed
- Sour cream (1/2 cup), fat-free
- Flour (1/3 cup)
- Skim milk (4 cups)
- Pepper (1/2 tsp)

Instructions

- Roast the potatoes in the oven or bake them at 400°F until tender.

- Let them cool before slicing them lengthwise and scooping out the pulp.
- Cook the flour over medium heat until it turns a light brown color, then slowly pour in the milk, stirring constantly until thoroughly combined.
- Add the pepper and potato pulp and mix well.
- Boil, stirring constantly, over medium heat until it is bubbly and thick.
- Mix in the cheese until it is fully melted.
- Remove the skillet from the heat and add the sour cream to it.

Turkey Broth

Time: 2 Hours and 30 Mins, Serves: 8, Skill: Hard

Ingredients

- Water (16 cups)
- Celery (2 stalks)
- Carrots (2)
- Onion (2), quartered
- Bay leaves (2)
- Ground black pepper (1/2 tsp)
- Dried (1/2 tsp) or fresh thyme (4 stems)
- Turkey/turkey breast carcass (1 small)

Instructions

- In a large pot, combine all the ingredients.
- Bring to a simmer, then reduce to low heat and continue to simmer for 2 hours, stirring occasionally.
- Remove the foam from the stock.
- Remove the carrots, skin, and bones from the broth with a strainer.

Drink & Beverage Recipes

Apple Cup Cider
Time: 25 Mins, Serves: 4, Skill: Easy

Ingredients
- Cinnamon sticks (2)
- Whole cloves (1/2 tsp)
- Nutmeg (1 pinch)
- Allspice (1 tsp)
- Apple juice (2 quarts 100%)

Instructions
- In a large saucepan, heat the apple juice over medium-high heat.
- Add the remaining ingredients.
- Reduce to low heat after bringing to a low boil. Allow for a 10-minute "steeping" period.
- Pour the cider into a mug or thermos using the fine metal sieve.

Mixed Berry Protein Smoothie
Time: 12 Mins, Serves: 2, Skill: Easy

Ingredients
- Cream topping (1/2 cup), whipped
- Whey protein powder (2 scoops)
- Coldwater (4 oz.)
- Mixed berries (1 cup), fresh/frozen
- Ice cubes (2)
- Crystal Light (1 tsp), flavor enhancer drops (liquid, any berry flavor)

Instructions
- Combine all the ingredients in a blender until creamy.
- Load the protein powder into a broad mixing cup.
- Stir in the cream topping thoroughly.

Lemonade
Time: 10 Mins, Serves: 2, Skill: Easy

Ingredients
- Ice cubes
- Water (2-1/2 cups)
- Sugar (1-1/4 cups)
- Lemon (1/2 tsp), finely shredded
- Fresh lemon or lime juice (1-1/4 cups)

Instructions
- Heat the water and sugar in a medium saucepan until the sugar has dissolved. Remove the pan from the heat and put it aside to cool for 20 minutes.
- In a large mixing cup, combine the lemon peel and juice. Allow to cool in a covered pitcher or pot. This can be held for up to three days.
- In a glass packed with ice, combine 3 oz. of base and 3 oz. of water to make a lemonade cocktail. Shake it up a little and serve.

Lemon-Strawberry Punch
Time: 10 Mins, Serves: 1, Skill: Easy

Ingredients
- Ginger ale (1 l. bottle)
- Lemonade concentrate (3cans), frozen, thawed
- Frozen strawberries (1 box 10 oz), in a light syrup, undrained and thawed

Instructions
- Whisk together the lemonade concentrate and 9 cans of water in a four-quart tub until well mixed.
- Fill a punch bowl halfway of lemonade. Strawberries may be combined in a number of ways.
- Apply the ice and ginger ale and whisk softly.

Vegan Hot Chocolate
Time: 15 Mins, Serves: 1, Skill: Easy

Ingredients
- Vanilla extract (1/2 tsp)
- Oat milk (1 cup)
- Cocoa powder (1 tbsp)
- Honey (2 tsp)

Instructions
- Heat the milk in a small saucepan over medium-high heat.

- Combine the cocoa powder, vanilla extract, and honey in a mixing cup.
- To mix, carefully whisk all the products together.
- Carry to a simmer before scalding (when bubbles emerge along the edges of the liquid in the pot).
- Extract it from the pan, put it into a mug, and serve.

Mexican Coconut Drink
Time: 25 Mins, Serves: 6, Skill: Easy

Ingredients
- Lime (4 slices)
- Water (2 cups)
- White rice (2 cups)
- Coconut water (2 cups), unsweetened
- Coconut milk (1 can), unsweetened
- Sugar (1/3 cup)

Instructions
- Fill a saucepan halfway with water (2 cups), bring to a boil, and remove from heat as soon as possible.
- In a medium mixing bowl, combine the coconut water and rice; cover and set aside at room temperature for the night.
- Blend the rice and coconut water mixture until smooth the next day.
- Wrap a medium-sized dish in cheesecloth and secure it with a rubber band or twine.
- Using cheesecloth, strain the liquid from the rice puree.
- Pour the rice water into a strainer and discard the rice sediment.
- In a small saucepan, heat the coconut milk and sugar over low heat for 4 minutes, or until the sugar is fully dissolved.
- Pour the sweetened coconut mixture over the rice and chill before ready to serve.

- Serve with ice and lime juice, garnished with lime slices.

Fruity Baked Tea
Time: 45 Mins, Serves: 1, Skill: Medium

Ingredients
- Apricots (1/2 cup), dried, diced
- Cloves (25 pieces)
- Star anise (4 pieces)
- Apple (1), diced
- Pear (1), diced
- Orange (1), diced
- Lemon (1), diced
- Peaches (1 cup), diced
- Berries (2 cups), blackberries, raspberries, blueberries, cherries, diced
- Powdered cinnamon (2 tsp)
- Brown sugar (2 tbsp)

Instructions
- Arrange all of the fruits in a baking bowl. Stir in all of the sugar and spices.
- Cover the bowl in aluminum foil to keep it dry. Bake for 40 minutes, stirring after 10 to 15 minutes.
- Remove the foil and bake for another 20 minutes to evaporate any juices and concentrate the taste.
- Extract the dish from the oven and automatically put the contents into four 8-ounce jars, or sixteen 2-ounce jars.
- Firmly seal the jars and encourage them to cool by standing on their lids with their bottoms up.
- Fill a medium saucepan halfway with water and bring to a boil. Boil for 15 minutes after inserting the bottoms of the jars.
- Remove the jars from the oven and put them aside to cool before placing them in the refrigerator.

- To serve, place 1 tablespoon of the mixture in a cup. Combine 8 oz. of boiling water in a glass and drink.

Strawberry Sesame Milkshake
Time: 16 Mins, Serves: 3, Skill: Easy

Ingredients
- Ice cubes (1 cup)
- Sesame seeds (1/2 tbsp), toasted
- Strawberries (1 lb.), halved
- Balsamic glaze (2 tbsp)
- Banana (1/2 small/50 grams), frozen, optional
- Coconut milk (1/2 cup)
- Tahini (2 tbsp)

Instructions
- Preheat the oven to 400 °F.
- In a mixing bowl, toss the strawberries with the balsamic glaze.
- Spread it out on a baking dish lined with parchment paper and set aside for 5 minutes.
- Cook for 10 minutes, then remove from the oven and flip the strawberries over to roast for another 10 minutes, or until softened.
- In a blender, combine the strawberries, coconut milk, tahini, pineapple, and ice and blend until smooth.
- Pour the smoothies into three glasses and top with toasted sesame seeds and a dry strawberry.

Rhubarb Tea
Time: 1 hour and 20 Mins, Serves: 8, Skill: Hard

Ingredients
- Mint, to garnish
- Rhubarb stalks (8)
- Water (8 cups)
- Sugar (1/3 cup)

Instructions
- Cut 8 rhubarb stalks into 3" sections, put in a pot of 8 cups water, bring to a boil, then reduce to low heat, and simmer for 1 hour.

Strain the drink, then apply about a third of a cup (or to taste) of sugar and put aside to cool.

Green Kiwi Smoothie
Time: 10 Mins, Serves: 1, Skill: Easy

Ingredients
- Water (1 cup)
- Honey (1 tsp), optional
- Kiwi (1), peeled, chopped
- Kale (1/2 cup), fresh or frozen, stemmed & chopped
- Almonds (2 tbsp)
- Ice cubes (2)

Instructions
- Add all the ingredients in a blender and mix until smooth.

Scarlet Frozen Fantasy
Time: 15 Mins, Serves: 2, Skill: Easy

Ingredients
- Cranberry (1 cup), juice cocktail
- Strawberries (1 cup), fresh, whole, washed and hulled
- Strawberries, for garnish
- Sugar (1/4 cup)
- Lime juice (2 tbsp), fresh
- Ice cubes (8-9)

Instructions
- In a mixer, combine the strawberries, cranberry juice, sugar, and lime juice. All can be carefully combined.
- Add ice cubes into the mix. Blend until fully smooth.
- Pour the mixture into chilled cups. Serve with a garnish of strawberries.

Zippy Dip
Time: 15 Mins, Serves: 2, Skill: Easy

Ingredients
- Green onion (3 tbsp), chopped

- Cayenne pepper (dash)
- Cream cheese (1 package 8 oz.), softened
- Margarine (1/2 cup), softened
- Mayonnaise (2 tbsp)
- Lemon juice (1 1/2 tsp)
- Hot dry mustard (1 1/2 tsp)
- Vinegar (1 tbsp)
- Horseradish (1 tsp)
- Paprika (1 tsp)
- Tarragon (1/2 tsp)
- Garlic powder (1/2 tsp)

Instructions

- In a blender, combine all ingredients and mix until smooth.
- Serve with new veggies or unsalted crackers.

Coffee Creamer
Time: 15 Mins, Serves: 4, Skill: Easy

Ingredients

- Milk (2 cups)
- Condensed milk (1 can x 14 oz.), sweetened

Added options

- Almond extract (1 tsp)
- Cocoa powder (2 tsp)
- Vanilla extract (2 tsp)
- Ice cream topping (2 tbsp), caramel
- Raspberry syrup (2 tbsp)

Instructions

- Combine the milk and condensed sweetened milk in a 32-ounce mixing cup.

- Apply the flavoring and whisk thoroughly.

Blueberry Protein Smoothie
Time: 10 Mins, Serves: 1, Skill: Easy

Ingredients

- Ice cubes (2), optional
- Whey protein powder (1 scoop), vanilla flavor
- Blueberry sherbet (1 cup), frozen
- Water (1/2 cup)

Instructions

- Add whey protein powder, frozen blueberry, and water in a blender (with ice cubes if desired).
- Mix for 30 to 45 seconds before serving.

Homemade Rice Milk
Time: 25 Mins, Serves: 2, Skill: Easy

Ingredients

- White rice (1 cup), cooked
- Filtered water (4 cups)

Instructions

- Combine the water and rice in a blender or food processor and blend for about 4 minutes, or until fluffy and smooth.
- Squeeze the remaining rice meal onto the fabric to collect the moisture, then pour the rice milk into a container using a double cheesecloth sheet or a strong sieve.
- Discard the rice meal and refrigerate the rice milk for up to one week in a lined glass jar.

Dessert Recipes

Sugarless Pecan and Raisin Cookies
Time: 55 Mins, Serves: 8, Skill: Medium

Ingredients
- Salt (1/2 tsp)
- Oil (1/4 cup)
- Egg (1)
- Pecans (1/2 cup)
- Raisins (1/2 cup)
- Flour (3/4 cup)
- Baking powder (2 tsp)
- Cinnamon (1/2 tsp)
- Canned orange juice (3/4 cup), unsweetened
- Orange rind (1/2 tsp)

Instructions
- In a big mixing bowl, combine the flour, baking powder, salt, and cinnamon.
- Add and combine the remaining ingredients.
- Drop by the teaspoonful onto a baking sheet that hasn't been greased.
- Preheat oven to 375°F and bake for 15 to 20 minutes.

Crispy Butterscotch Cookies
Time: 40 Mins, Serves: 10, Skill: Easy

Ingredients
- Sugar (1/2 cup)
- Egg alternative (3 tbsp)
- Milk (1 tbsp)
- Vanilla extract (1 tsp)
- Margarine (1/2 cup)
- Packed brown sugar (1/2 cup)
- Cream of Wheat (1 cup)
- Butterscotch chips (1 cup)
- All-purpose flour (1 cup + 3 tbsp)
- Baking powder (1 tsp)
- Cinnamon (1/2 tsp), ground

Instructions
- Preheat the oven to 350 °F.
- In a mixing tub, cream together the sugar and butter.
- Add and whisk together the egg, chocolate, and milk. Using a blender, soften the mixture.
- In a mixing cup, combine the flour, cinnamon, and baking powder.
- Pour into the butter mixture and whisk well.
- Add in the butterscotch chips and cereal thoroughly.
- Drop teaspoons one at a time onto the prepared baking dish.
- Bake for 9–12 minutes, or until golden brown.
- Allow to cool on the baking sheet for 1 minute before switching to cooling racks.

Easy Spicy Angel Cake
Time: 40 Mins, Serves: 18, Skill: Easy

Ingredients
- Nutmeg (1/2 tsp), ground
- Ginger (1/4 tsp), ground
- Cloves (1/4 tsp), ground
- Angel food cake mix (1 pkg)
- Cinnamon (1 tsp), ground

Instructions
- In a bowl, combine all the ingredients.
- Begin cooking and baking as directed on the box.
- Set aside to cool.
- Cut each segment into one-inch pieces.
- Include a whipped topping and strawberry or pineapple to finish.

Chocolate Covered Strawberries
Time: 25 Mins, Serves: 2, Skill: Easy

Ingredients
- Corn syrup (1 tbsp)
- Margarine (5 tbsp)
- Strawberries (1 qtr.)
- Chocolate chips (1/2 cup), semi-sweet

Instructions

- Over a low flame, melt the first three ingredients.
- Blend until fully smooth.
- Switch off the heat and cover the pan with water.
- Put strawberries on waxed paper after dipping them in chocolate.
- Place the food in the fridge to cool before serving.

Apple Filled Crepes
Time: 30 Mins, Serves: 6, Skill: Easy

Ingredients

- Eggs (2)
- Sugar (1/2 cup)
- Flour (1 cup)
- Oil (1/4 cup)
- Milk (2 cups)
- Egg yolks (4)
- Apples (4 pieces)
- Brown sugar (1/2 cup)
- Cinnamon (1/2 tsp)
- Nutmeg (1/2 tsp)
- Butter (1 stick or 1/2 cup), unsalted

Instructions

- Whisk together the egg yolks, entire whites, sugar, flour, butter, and milk in a big mixing bowl until smooth.
- In a tiny nonstick pan, melt the oil over medium heat.
- Coat the bowl with nonstick cooking spray.
- Spoon 1 scoop of batter into the tub with a 2-ounce ladle or 1/4 cup, and roll the pan to evenly scatter the crepe batter on the bottom.
- Cook for 20 seconds, on one side, then flip and cook for another 10 seconds on the other. While we prepare the filling, set the crepes aside.
- Peel and core the apples, and cut them into 12 slices each.

- Steam the apples in a medium sauté pan.
- Eventually, apply the brown sugar to the melting butter.
- In a mixing dish, combine the cinnamon, apples, and nutmeg.
- Cook until the apples are tender but not soggy. Remove from the heat and set aside to cool.
- Fill each crepe's center with approximately two tablespoons of apple filling.

Apple Oat Shake
Time: 30 Mins, Serves: 4, Skill: Easy

Ingredients

- Wheat germ (1 tbsp)
- Vanilla extract (1 1/2 tsp)
- Frozen apple (1/2 pieces), cut into chunks
- Oatmeal (1/2 cup), cooked, chilled
- Skim milk (2/3 cup)
- Brown sugar (2 tbsp)

Instructions

- Blend the oatmeal for a couple minutes in a blender.
- In a large mixing cup, whisk together the milk, vanilla, brown sugar, wheat germ, and half of the apple mixture.
- Blend until the mixture has reached a creamy, dense consistency.

Blueberry Whipped Pie
Time: 1 hour and 30 Mins, Serves: 9, Skill: Medium

Ingredients

- Graham cracker crumbs (2 cups)
- Cinnamon (1 tsp)
- Granulated sugar (1/4 cup)
- Lemon juice (2 tsp)
- Vanilla extract (1 tsp)
- Whipped cream (8 oz. tub), non-dairy
- Blueberries (3 cups)
- Butter (1/2 cup), melted, unsalted
- Cream cheese (8 oz.), softened

Instructions

- Preheat oven to 375°F.
- Put the cinnamon sticks, graham cracker crumbs, and melted butter in a medium mixing cup.
- To make a crust, thinly scatter the mixture in the bottom of a 9-inch circular or square baking dish.
- After baking, allow for 7 minutes of cooking time.
- In a big mixing tub, using a hand processor, smooth out the melted cream cheese.
- In a mixing cup, combine the vanilla and lemon juice.
- Before applying the blueberries, fold in the whipped topping softly.
- Cover the whole surface with the paste.
- After covering, place in the refrigerator for at least 1 hour.

Molten Mint Chocolate Brownies

Time: 40 Mins, Serves: 8, Skill: Easy

Ingredients

- Andes mint chocolates (12 pieces)
- Optional garnish: cocoa powder, powdered sugar, fresh mint springs,
- Betty Crocker brownie mix (1 box)

Instructions

- Preheat the oven to 350°F and follow the product instructions for cooking the brownie mix.
- In a 12-cup muffin pan that has been lined or lightly oiled, flour the bottom sheet. Bake for 25 minutes after putting the brownie mix in the pans.
- After placing one slice of mint candy in the middle, bake for an additional 5 minutes. Remove the brownies from the oven and place them on a cooling rack to cool. Allow for 5–10 minutes of cooling before serving.

Yellow Cake

Time: 1 hour and 25 Mins, Serves: 8, Skill: Medium

Ingredients

- Sugar (2/3 cup)
- Water (1/2 cup)
- Egg (1)
- Vanilla (1/2 tsp)
- Master Mix (1 1/2 cups)

Instructions

- Preheat the oven to 375 °F.
- For Master Mix, follow the steps outlined.
- Add some sugar to the mixture.
- In a separate dish, whisk together the egg, water, and vanilla extract.
- Beat for 2 minutes after adding half of the solvent to the mixture.
- Pour in the remaining liquid and continue to beat for 2 minutes.
- Bake for 25 minutes in a tray lined with wax paper.
- One 8-inch layer is made for this recipe.

Tropical Fruit Salad with Basil Lime Syrup

Time: 1 hour and 10 Mins, Serves: 10, Skill: Medium

Ingredients

- Strawberries (1 1/2 cup), sliced
- Mango (1 cup), cubed
- Pineapple (2 cups), cubed
- Water (1/4 cup)
- Sugar (1/4 cup)
- Lime zest (1 1/2 tsp)
- Packed basil leaves (1/4 cup)

Instructions

- Bring water to a boil in a small frying pan and stir in sugar.
- Boil and cook until the sugar melts.
- Take the pan off the heat and stir in the lime zest and basil.

- In a large mixing cup, combine the fruits while the syrup cools.
- Soak the cheesecloth or strainer in the syrup to remove the solids.
- Serve as a side dish of fruits or as a snack.

Vanilla Strudel

Time: 1 hour and 40 Mins, Serves: 12, Skill: Hard

Ingredients

- Vanilla extract (1 tsp)
- Sugar (4 tbsp)
- Cinnamon (1/2 tsp), ground
- Butter (4 tbsp), unsalted
- Phyllo dough (12 sheets)
- Pumpkin (1 1/2 cups), unsweetened
- Nutmeg (1/2 tsp), grated

Instructions

- Preheat the oven to 380 °F. Place an oven shelf in the oven's middle.
- Whisk together the pumpkin, nutmeg, vanilla extract, 12 tablespoons of cinnamon, and 2 teaspoons of sugar in a medium mixing cup until well mixed.
- Butter a medium non-stick baking tray with a pastry knife. On a smooth work surface, spread a sheet of basic phyllo dough and cover with butter. Then, one by one, stack the buttered phyllo tubes, coating each one with melted butter. Before using the leftover phyllo sheets, cover them in foil wrap.
- After completed all 12 sheets, scatter the mixture uniformly on one of the stack's longer sides. Begin rolling from the filling edge to a blank end, seam-side down.
- Place the roll, seam-side down, on the oiled sheet plate, and dust with the remaining butter.
- In a small cup, combine the remaining cinnamon and sugar. Distribute it evenly over the top and sides of the strudel.
- Bake for 12 to 15 minutes on the center rack of the oven, until well browned.
- Remove the baked strudel from the oven and put it aside for 5 to 10 minutes.
- Enable the center to cool before cutting and serving with a sharp knife.

Cornbread Muffins

Time: 1 hour, Serves: 12, Skill: Easy

Ingredients

- Sugar (1/4 cup)
- Baking powder (2 tsp)
- Liquid egg substitute (1/2 cup)
- Rice milk (1 cup), unenriched
- Butter (2 tbsp), unsalted
- All-purpose white flour (1 cup)
- Plain cornmeal (1 cup)

Instructions

- Preheat the oven to 400 °F.
- Combine the flour, sugar, cornmeal, and baking powder in a mixing dish.
- Whisk together the egg substitute, melted butter, and rice milk in a separate container.
- Combine the dry and wet products just after they've been moistened.
- Fill muffin cups halfway. In oiled or paper-lined muffin tins, pour 2/3 of the batter.
- Bake for 15–20 minutes, or when a toothpick inserted in the center comes out clean.
- Serve immediately.

Reduced Sugar Carrot Cupcakes

Time: 1 hour and 35 Mins, Serves: 16, Skill: Hard

Ingredients

- Mixed spice (2 tsp)
- Orange (1)
- Eggs (2)
- Sunflower oil (150ml)
- Carrots (200g)
- Light muscovado sugar (125g)

- Whole meal flour (100g)
- White flour (50g)
- Bicarbonate of soda (1 tsp)

Icing
- Butter (70g), softened
- Soft cheese (200g), low fat
- Vanilla extract (1/2 tsp)
- Icing sugar (50g), sifted

Instructions
- Preheat the oven to 350 °F and line 12 muffin tins with paper liners.
- In a mixing cup, combine the flour, mixed seasoning, bicarbonate of soda, and orange zest.
- In a separate cup, whisk together the eggs, oil, and sugar, then stir them into the dry ingredients. Grated and peeled carrots should be added to the mixture and thoroughly blended in.
- Put the mixture into the muffin tins and bake for 20-22 minutes, or until a skewer inserted in the middle comes out clean. After that, set it aside to cool on a wire rack.
- Melt the butter, and add the soft cheese, sifted icing sugar, and vanilla extract to produce the icing. Using a palette/cutlery knife, swirl icing on top of cakes.

Chocolate profiteroles with Chantilly cream
Time: 1 hour, Serves: 8, Skill: Easy

Ingredients
Profiteroles
- Eggs (2 medium)
- Plain flour (75g)
- Coldwater (150ml)
- Butter (50g), unsalted

Chantilly cream
- Vanilla extract (1 tsp)
- Double cream (300ml)
- Caster sugar (1 tbsp)

Chocolate sauce
- Dark chocolate (100g)

Instructions
- Preheat the oven to 338 °F, and lightly grease a baking sheet (non-stick). Sift the flour into a mixing cup. Bring water and diced butter to a boil in a large saucepan.
- Slowly drizzle in the flour until the paste clings to the whisk. Replace the whisk with a wooden spoon and stir for 2-3 minutes, or before it comes away from the pan's sides and falls off a spoon.
- Take it off the burner. Beat in the eggs one at a time. Combine the ingredients with a wooden spoon or an electric whisk. The finished product should be smooth and polished.
- Using a dessert spoon/ piping bag with a 1 cm nozzle, pipe 18 equal-sized balls of pastry onto a baking tray. Preheat oven to 180°F and bake for 18-20 minutes, or until golden and puffy. Remove it from the oven and set it aside to cool until its done cooking.
- To make Chantilly cream, add cream, sugar, and vanilla extract in a mixing cup. Combine them with an electric whisk or a hand whisk to form soft peaks. Cut a slit in each profiterole with a nozzle, then pipe cream filling into each one.
- To melt the chocolate, break it up and drop it in a heatproof bowl set over a pan of simmering water (do not let the bowl touch the water). Serve molten chocolate profiteroles with a drizzle of melted chocolate on top.

Dutch Apple Pancake
Time: 45 Mins, Serves: 4, Skill: Easy

Ingredients
- Eggs (3)
- All-purpose flour (1/2 cup)
- Milk (1/2 cup)
- Sour cream (1 tbsp)
- Salt (1/4 tsp)

- Butter (2 tbsp), unsalted
- Granny Smith apples (3 large)
- Granulated sugar (6 tbsp)
- Cinnamon (1 tsp), ground
- Lemon zest (1 tsp), grated

Instructions

- Melt the butter in an oven-safe tub over medium-high heat.
- Add the apples, sugar, and cinnamon and simmer, stirring regularly, for 3-5 minutes.
- Whisk the eggs in a cup until foamy. In a mixing dish, combine the flour, cinnamon, sour cream, zest, and juice.
- Combine all the ingredients in a mixing bowl so they form a batter-like consistency.
- Pour over apples and bake at 400°F for 25 minutes, or until mildly puffed and orange.
- Slice into wedges and serve straight away.

Conclusion

You have been given all the tools you might need, so as to learn all there is to know about intermittent fasting over the age of 50. Now it is all up to you. You should know by now how valuable this type of feeding rotation can be for you, especially as you are growing older. It is not just about shedding some extra pounds or boosting your metabolism. It is also about increasing your lifespan, making you feel healthier and more content about things that happen every day. This is a once-in-a-lifetime opportunity to reset your body and literally start over. Don't you want this transformation?

This is just the beginning of the journey. You might feel anxious, a little overwhelmed by information and eager to see what lies ahead. Don't be in a hurry. Let the journey take you where you want to be, offering you amazing benefits throughout the whole process. After all, it is a work in progress. As you dive deeper, you get to realize more details about intermittent fasting. You discover more things about the way your own body works and responds to different situations. Over time, you comprehend which foods are good for you and which ones you should omit from your diet plan. And as you see that transformation slowly taking place, your determination becomes stronger. It is fascinating, learning to interpret the signs and allowing your body to heal itself.

Do not just choose to fast without first reading all about it. This would be a disaster. You should know by now your body is complex, with various layers in need of exploration. So, give yourself some time to study and realize what is best for you in the long run. Turn to science, whenever you are experiencing even the slightest sliver of doubt. Do not let it simmer, as it is going to grow into an even more important issue over time. Clear the air, let nothing unanswered, and when you are ready, ease yourself into the process of intermittent fasting.

I hope this book has been inspirational in your journey, which is about to start now. I wish you all the best, and I am looking forward to the revolutionary changes which are about to take place in your life. It is an exciting thing to see people who have chosen intermittent fasting, as they are changing from within. They look radiant, totally transformed and filled with hope for the future.

Thanks for reading this book.

I would be extremely grateful if you would take 1 minute of your time to leave a review on Amazon about my work.

Amber Lane

Customer reviews

★★★★★ 4.9 out of 5

44 global ratings

5 star		90%
4 star		10%
3 star		0%
2 star		0%
1 star		0%

˅ How are ratings calculated?

SCAN ME

Made in the USA
Monee, IL
27 March 2022